"*Inspirational*. The authors of this collection of short, anecdotal stories range from a survivor of the Bataan Death March to the mother of the leader of the U.S. Air Force Demonstration Team—the Thunderbirds. When your faith in the human spirit is at a low ebb, read a few of these stories and your faith will be restored. I guarantee it."

DONALD S. LOPEZ, LT. COL. USAF (RETIRED)

"In *Stories from a Soldier's Heart*, Alice Gray and Chuck Holton make your spirit soar. These true stories reveal the politically incorrect truth about real war stories—atheism does not survive the reality of war. Soldiers who face battle must confront their relationship with God. Warriors who follow Christ into battle testify to others of His saving grace. These true-to-life episodes are good stories well told."

JAMES BLACKWELL, MILITARY ANALYST TO THE PENTAGON,
CNN, AND FOX NEWS

THE STORIES FOR THE HEART COLLECTION

Stories for the Heart, The Original Collection
Stories for the Heart, The Second Collection
Stories for the Heart, The Third Collection
Stories for a Woman's Heart
Stories for a Woman's Heart, The Second Collection
Stories for a Teen's Heart, Book 1
Stories for a Teen's Heart, Book 2
Stories for a Teen's Heart, Book 3
Stories for the Family's Heart
Stories for a Man's Heart
Stories for a Faithful Heart
Stories for the Extreme Teen's Heart
Christmas Stories for the Heart
Stories for a Cheerful Heart
Stories for a Mom's Heart
Stories for a Dad's Heart
Stories for the Romantic Heart
Stories for the Teacher's Heart
Stories for a Grad's Heart

ALSO BY ALICE GRAY
The Fragrance of Friendship
A Pleasant Place
Morning Coffee and Time Alone
Quiet Moments and a Cup of Tea
Gentle Is a Grandmother's Love
Once Upon a Christmas

ALSO BY CHUCK HOLTON
A More Elite Soldier (July 2003)

STORIES
from a
SOLDIER'S
HEART

Compiled by
ALICE GRAY *and* CHUCK HOLTON

Multnomah Books

STORIES FROM A SOLDIER'S HEART
published by Multnomah Books
A division of Random House, Inc.

© 2003 by Multnomah Publishers
International Standard Book Number: 1-59052-307-5

cover design by Steve Gardner
image of flag by Photo Disc,
image of soldiers by Department of Defense
Images on pages 5, 11, 28, 60, 125, 142, 151, 161, 188 by Corbis
Images on pages 83, 100, 199, 232 by Getty Images
Images on pages 41, 221, 233 by Department of Defense

Please see the acknowledgments at the back of the book for complete attribution for
material used in this book.

Unless otherwise indicated, Scripture quotations are from:
The Holy Bible, New International Version
© 1973, 1984 by International Bible Society,
used by permission of Zondervan Publishing House
Stories for the Heart is a trademark of Multnomah Publishers
and is registered in the U.S. Patent and Trademark Office

Multnomah is a trademark of Multnomah Publishers
and is registered in the U.S. Patent and Trademark Office.
The colophon is a trademark of Multnomah Publishers.

For information:
MULTNOMAH BOOKS
12265 ORACLE BOULEVARD, SUITE 200
COLORADO SPRINGS, CO 80921

09 10 11—9 8 7 6 5 4

$\star\star\star$

DEDICATED TO

America's heroes…one and all.

The men and women of the:
United States Air Force
United States Army
United States Coast Guard
United States Marine Corps
United States Navy

A Special Thank-You To

★★★

The authors who wrote wonderful stories
celebrating the men and women of the United States military.
This book isn't ours…it's yours.

The members of AWSA,
Advanced Writers and Speakers Association
The members of CLASS, Christian Leaders and Speakers Services
The attendees of the 2003 Mt. Hermon Writer's Conference
Members of Redland Baptist Church, Rockville, Maryland
You pulled together with us and volunteered your personal stories.
You are wonderful and your stories are incredible!

Ashley Blake, Jennifer Curley, Doug Gabbert,
Jennifer Gates, Steve Gardner, Pamela McGrew,
Brian Thomasson, and Gayle Vickery
You are the awesome team that pulled this
together at the eleventh hour.

Friends and family
Your prayers and encouragement kept us going.

Our heavenly Father
It's not the size of the mountain…
but the strength of the Mountain Mover.

CONTENTS

PATRIOTISM

DEDICATION AND COURAGE

HONOR AND SACRIFICE

LOVE AND FAMILY

INSPIRATION

FAITH ON THE FRONT LINES

BECAUSE WE CARE

PATRIOTISM

THE TREASURE·OF AMERICA

*The world is beginning to understand
why we treasure America so much—
our values, our freedom,
and the strength of the American character.*

PRESIDENT GEORGE W. BUSH

I PLEDGE ALLEGIANCE

★★★

CAPT. JOHN S. McCAIN, USN (RETIRED)
CURRENT U.S. SENATOR, ARIZONA

As you may know, I spent five and a half years as a prisoner of war during the Vietnam War. In the early years of our imprisonment, the NVA [North Vietnamese Army] kept us in solitary confinement or two or three to a cell. In 1971 the NVA moved us from these conditions of isolation into large rooms with as many as thirty to forty men to a room. This was, as you can imagine, a wonderful change and was a direct result of the efforts of millions of Americans on behalf of a few hundred POWs ten thousand miles from home.

One of the men who moved into my room was a young man named Mike Christian. Mike came from a small town near Selma, Alabama. He didn't wear a pair of shoes until he was thirteen years old. At seventeen, he enlisted in the U.S. Navy. He later earned a commission by going to Officer Training School. Then he became a naval flight officer and was shot down and captured in 1967.

Mike had a keen appreciation of the opportunities this country and our military provide for people who want to work and want to succeed. As part of the change in treatment, the Vietnamese allowed some prisoners to receive packages from home. In some of these packages were handkerchiefs, scarves, and other items of clothing. Mike got himself a bamboo needle. Over a period of a couple of months, he created an American flag and sewed it on the inside of his shirt. Every afternoon, before we had a bowl of soup, we would hang Mike's shirt on the wall of the cell and say the Pledge of Allegiance. I know the Pledge of Allegiance may not seem the most important part of our day now, but I can assure you that in that stark cell it was indeed the most important event.

One day the Vietnamese searched our cell, as they did periodically, and discovered Mike's shirt with the flag sewn inside and removed it. That evening they returned, opened the door of the cell, and for the benefit of all us, beat Mike Christian severely for the next couple of hours. Then they opened the door of the cell and threw him in.

We cleaned him up as well as we could. The cell in which we lived had a concrete slab in the middle on which we slept. Four naked light bulbs hung in each corner of the room. After the excitement died down, I looked in the corner of the room, and sitting there beneath that dim light bulb with a piece of red cloth, another shirt, and his bamboo needle, was my friend, Mike Christian. He was sitting there with his eyes almost shut from the beating he had received, making another American flag. He was not making the flag because it made Mike Christian feel better. He was making that flag because he knew how important it was to us to be able to pledge allegiance to our flag and our country.

So the next time you say the Pledge of Allegiance, you must never forget the sacrifice and courage that thousands of Americans have made to build our nation and promote freedom around the world. You must remember our duty, our honor, and our country.

"I pledge allegiance to the flag of the United States of America, and to the Republic for which it stands, one nation under God, indivisible, with liberty and justice for all."

DEDICATION TO DUTY

✯✯✯

AUTHOR UNKNOWN

A foreign diplomat who often criticized American policy observed a United States Marine perform the evening colors ceremony. The diplomat wrote about this simple but solemn ceremony in a letter to his country:

During one of the past few days, I had occasion to visit the U.S. embassy in our capital after official working hours. I arrived at a quarter to six and was met by the marine on guard at the entrance of the chancery. He asked if I would mind waiting while he lowered the two American flags at the embassy. What I witnessed over the next ten minutes so impressed me that I am now led to make this occurrence a part of my ongoing record of this distressing era.

The marine was dressed in a uniform which was spotless and neat; he walked with a measured tread from the entrance of the chancery to the stainless steel flagpole before the embassy and reverently lowered the flag to the level of his reach, where he began to fold it in military fashion.

He then released the flag from the clasps attaching it to the rope, stepped back from the pole, made an about face, and carried the flag between his hands—one above and one below—and placed it securely on a stand before the chancery. He then marched over to the second flagpole

15

and repeated the same lonesome ceremony. On the way between poles, he mentioned to me very briefly that he would soon be finished.

After completing his task, he apologized for the delay—out of pure courtesy, as nothing less than incapacity would have prevented him from fulfilling his goal—and said to me, "Thank you for waiting, Sir. I had to pay honor to my country."

I have had to tell this story because there was something impressive about a lone marine carrying out a ceremonial task which obviously meant very much to him and which, in its simplicity, made the might, the power, and the glory of the United States of America stand forth in a way that a mighty wave of military aircraft, or the passage of a super-carrier, or a parade of ten thousand men could never have.

In spite of all the many things that I can say negatively about the United States, I do not think there is a soldier, yea, even a private citizen, who could feel as proud about our country today as the marine does for his country.

One day it is my hope to visit one of our embassies in a faraway place and to see a soldier fold our flag and turn to a stranger and say, "I am sorry for the delay, Sir. I had to honor my country."

~

Liberty is not America's gift to the world,
it is God's gift to each and every human being.
So as we pursue peace, we also pursue liberty.

PRESIDENT GEORGE BUSH

THE GREATNESS OF AMERICA

ALEXIS DE TOCQUEVILLE

Early in the nineteenth century the French statesman, Alexander de Tocqueville, made a study of democracy in our country and wrote as follows...

I sought for the greatness and genius of America in her commodious harbors and her ample rivers, and it was not there.

I sought for the greatness and genius of America in her fertile fields and boundless forests, and it was not there.

I sought for the greatness and genius of America in her rich mines and her vast world commerce, and it was not there.

I sought for the greatness and genius of America in her public school system and her institutions of learning, and it was not there.

I sought for the greatness and genius of America in her democratic congress and her matchless constitution, and it was not there.

Not until I went into the churches of America and heard her pulpits flame with righteousness did I understand the secret of her genius and power.

America is great because America is good, and if America ever ceases to be good, America will cease to be great.

THE PATRIOT

★★★

KIM MEEDER
CONDENSED FROM *HOPE RISING*

Red, white, and blue decorations were strewn in every direction beneath the bright morning sun. It was almost time. After all the fluffing, combing, glittering, and painting, the kids and horses were nearly ready. I surveyed the aftermath of the happy onslaught. The sparkling debris on the ground made the earth itself shine with a dazzling grin. It was the best of days—it was the Fourth of July.

I wanted the kids to understand that this parade was not for them. It was to honor the brave souls in uniform whose service to our great land ensured our freedom. Only a few of those soldiers had survived to see this day; fewer still were able to celebrate with us in the parade. Today was *their* day.

I tried to explain to the children how much these brave men and women gave to protect their country, their homes, their families, and us. They did their job out of their sense of honor, and in return we show our honor out of respect and gratitude.

Quiet moments passed. Music and the clattering of hooves and creaking of wagons floated our way. It was nearly time to go. But there was one more thing that needed to be said.

"When you watch the fireworks tonight light up the sky, understand that every light, every single spark that ignites the darkness, burns hot and then burns out. Remember that each one represents a life that was given. A life that burned bright and then burned out so that you and I could be free. Freedom is not free. It has been earned for us by thousands who gave their all so that you and I could share in their victory. Our job today is to seek out the veterans who are here and thank them."

With full hearts we marched on to the parade route. Each horse could have been flown from a flagpole, so dazzling were their proud decorations. Jubilant, waving children sat astride their bannered backs, shining in head-to-toe patriotism. I walked out, leading my horse and her young rider into the last position.

We squeezed down the street between waving flags, and I looked for an opportunity to express my thanks personally to some of the veterans. Halfway through the parade, between the freckled faces and sticky-fingered waves, I saw him.

He sat in a wheelchair much too large for his frail body. His hands, crippled with age, were folded on his blanketed lap. His body was ravaged by time, but he proudly wore on his sagging white head a neatly creased olive drab cap with the unmistakable insignia of a World War II veteran.

With horse and child in tow I paused, trying to gain the old soldier's attention. I tipped my cowboy hat to him and said, "Thank you!"

His rheumy eyes came into focus and his head snapped up. His lips parted as he stared at me.

His eyebrows furrowed together as he tried to read the emotions on my face. He didn't seem to realize that I was talking just to him. I removed my hat and pressed it to my chest and looked directly into his eyes. "What you have done has not been forgotten."

For a second his face contorted with the pain of long-suppressed memories. And then a torrent of tears flooded his weathered cheeks. He dropped his face into his cupped hands. His shoulders crumpled forward. One sob after another shook his frail body. I watched him over my shoulder until a shifting crowd of devoted well-wishers enveloped him.

Wow, Lord! What just happened? I moved on down the parade route. My intent had been to honor the veteran, not to crush him beneath a wave of grief. My heart was devastated. Had I inadvertently ripped open an ancient scar? Or had his thoughts flashed back to a foreign battlefield where he watched as his brothers' lives had flamed with staggering passion, burned bright, and then were burned out before him?

The parade drew to a close and our entourage returned to its staging area where everyone was abuzz about their many adventures during the trip down Main Street. I was so proud of them all. Clearly they had understood the message I'd tried to communicate to them before the parade. And with childlike innocence they had carried it out.

"Kim!" One of the parents called to me.

He waved me over and told me he had been standing near the veteran. The elderly man continued to quietly weep, evidently consumed by his private grief. Then he drew out a worn handkerchief, used it to dry his face, and carefully returned it to his pocket. The man moved his shoulders back until they rested firmly against his chair. He moved his once-hanging head back and up until he held it at military attention between his squared shoulders.

My friend's description of what he had seen reflected my exact thoughts: True patriotism is not confined or diminished by age.

Within my heart is a vault of heroes. Some are as close as my own soul; some I have never met. When I think of him now, the patriot, I will always remember him as one of their treasured number—someone who inspires me to become a better person. I will always remember him as my hero.

HIDDEN HEROES

★ ★ ★

ELLIE KAY

During the final days of the Gulf War, I took our three-year-old son, Daniel, his two-year-old brother, Philip, and our infant daughter, Bethany, to watch their father launch in his F-4 Phantom. He was going to the Middle East. His mission: to fight for our nation's freedom.

"When will Papa be back home, Mama?" asked Daniel as he waved his chubby hand at the airplane.

"Soon," I said as I fought back the tears and kissed my baby daughter on her fuzzy blonde head. "We are praying he will come home soon."

Philip was excited, he loved watching airplanes. "I wuv you, Papa!" he shouted as he jumped up and down. All of the sudden, he turned to me, furrowed his brow and said very seriously, "You know, I weally wuv de Papa." Then he turned to wave at the small speck in the sky as his dad flew his mission.

The children didn't quite understand what their father did for a living a decade ago, but after the Kosovo war and now with our current situation—they do. As a military family who currently has five school-aged children and two adult children, we have a keen appreciation of what it takes to keep this nation free. We've lived through these two wars and know that my husband will likely be called upon again to fly and fight in order to protect our nation's freedoms. We're the veterans on the homefront.

Some have called military families the "hidden heroes at home," but most of us would not accept such a distinction. After all, we don't wear the uniform, we haven't taken the oath to offer our life's blood to defend our nation, we don't eat MRE rations in some faraway place. We merely support those who do.

~

Men who have offered their lives for
their country know that patriotism is not
the fear of something,
it is the love of something.

ADLAI STEVENSON

A TWENTY-ONE-DAY FLAG SALUTE

DAVID B. COLEMAN, NC1(SW), USN (RETIRED)

On a quiet, tree-lined street, just at the break of dawn, there was a slight breeze blowing. Some houses had lights on with their occupants stirring about while others were still dark and quiet. The door to one of the lit homes opened and Alice, a small, elderly woman, quietly hung her American flag on the post of her front porch. Her little dog, Ginger, ran out to sniff around the flower beds where the roses lifted their fragrance to the morning sun. She watched her flag for a moment as it caught the morning breeze. Satisfaction played across her face as she smiled. Alice called to Ginger who followed her back inside. The door closed to the simple but well-kept home. No one else was out moving about at this time of the morning, and no one witnessed this patriotic event except maybe the paperboy as he rode past on his bike. Seeing her flag would remind him that today was Flag Day.

Alice was a widow whose only companion was her small dog. This annual habit served as a silent testament to her fierce patriotism. It was not anything flashy or brassy, and she did it without being asked. She did it out of love of country, respect for our great land, and because it was something she had the ability to do.

These days, it is not unusual to see American flags hanging from porches and next to the door posts of many homes. Some even have proper flagpoles erected in their yards to prominently display Old Glory year around. There are those blessed ones who did not need the prompting of a terrible tragedy to show their love of country. Long before the tragedy of September 11, 2001, she set out her American flag at sunrise every June 14 for Flag Day and took it down at sunset. She did this every day up to July 4, Independence Day, when at sunset she would retire those colors until the next patriotic holiday. When asked about it, she would smile and say it was her "twenty-one-day salute." This display of patriotism is how she viewed her grand tribute to the land she loved.

This tribute of hers was borne out of a long-standing love of her country and out of a simple pride of being an American. It was her way of saying thank you to the many men and women who wore her country's uniforms and went in harm's way to protect her and her country's way of life. Those seven red stripes, six white stripes, and fifty white stars on a field of dark blue held more meaning for her than just a simple flag. It was this deep-seated meaning that stirred her to fly her flag every year on Flag Day, a symbol that, at this house, there was one who would not forget the sacrifices made by many for her to be able to have the blessings and freedom she enjoyed.

A simple house on a quiet, tree-lined street with one very patriotic and faithful citizen who chose to remember and, by her faithful efforts, remind the rest of us, too.

Alice's daughter is the one who told me this story. Having spent twenty years in the service of our country, many of those years at sea or overseas, it was comforting to know that there were such people back home. People like Alice who live in homes on tree-lined streets in towns across America. Simple folk who were behind us and supported us for the job we were doing. The time I served in the navy was never done to earn anyone's thanks, and the few times that people did thank me for defending our country always left me feeling a bit surprised and humbled. To Alice, who has gone on to be with her Lord, and to Bob, her grandson, whom Alice left the flag with and who now flies it 24/7, and to others like them…thank you from one who was proud to go in harm's way for you and our way of life.

A RADICAL
RECONSIDERS

BARBARA CURTIS

For a young woman seeking the counterculture's cutting edge, I was in the right place at the right time: Washington, D.C., as the sixties rolled into the seventies. For too long I believed we were the bravest and the best.

Milling outside the Pentagon chanting, "One, two, three, four/We don't want your bloody war!/Ho, Ho, Ho Chi Minh/Viet Cong are going to win!" Disrupting bridges during rush hour, banners waving. If the government won't stop the war, we'll stop the government. Retreating under clouds of tear gas, some of us hauled to jail.

That I didn't really know anyone in the service made it all too easy to feel superior. I was young, my thinking was sloppy, my judgments unyielding. That it took over two decades for me to see my folly might seem remarkable. But let's face it: despite its self-anointing as the Generation of Peace and Love, the counterculture could be quite dogmatic, callous, and cruel. Think of our music, riddled with elitism and scorn for those we despised.

It's time to right that wrong. Time to deal with the disconnect many in my generation had with the reality of war and peace. Time to acknowledge that our fixation on the ambiguities of Vietnam—as well our extreme narcissism—truly undercut our appreciation of the heroism displayed by those who served their country.

In 1999, I was fortunate to meet one of these unsung heroes. As two of the youngest guests at a dinner party, my husband and I listened in awe as seventy-somethings swapped stories of World War II days.

Later, I interviewed one, a former first lieutenant who makes his home in Petaluma, California.

Tom Mooney received his wings as an Army Air Corps bomber pilot in 1944, with just time enough to marry his high-school sweetheart before going overseas. Kit and her mother traveled from their hometown of St. Louis for a California wedding. Tom's crew served as the wedding party before the ten men boarded their B-24 Liberator at Hamilton Air Force Base.

"Our orders were secret until a certain altitude," Tom told me. "When we opened them, we found our final destination was Wales, where we spent some time in orientation—eating lots of good country eggs, bacon, and milk—before being stationed in Norwich, forty-five miles north of London."

Tom's first mission, in August 1944, was to Karlsruhe, Germany, right off the French border. The crew had heard this was a "milk run," because it took them across Allied-occupied territory. They came back with 345 holes in their plane.

"All I could think was that if this was a milk run, what would it be like when we have to go to Munich or Hamburg?" Tom says.

When Tom's crew arrived in Norwich, standard operating procedure was this: After twenty bombing missions, if a man was still alive, he was sent home, his tour of duty complete. But the army kept upping the ante—to twenty-five, thirty, and finally thirty-five missions. That's how many Tom Mooney flew in his eight months at Norwich.

What was his scariest flight?

"Our twelfth," he answers without hesitation. "We were going in over the north end of the Rhine when we lost an engine. We were able to keep up with the formation with only three, but then we lost another. We headed for Holland, where we dropped our bomb load safe, then on over Belgium and France.

"We crash-landed at Lille. Our descent was so fast there was an inch-and-a-half of ice on the plane, including the windshield. I had to open the window and stick my head out to see. I was standing with my body weight on full rudder."

Tom came back to the States and his wife and went on to earn an M.A. in history at Brown University. Now a retired Boy Scouts executive and recent widower, he is an active father and grandfather with two children and five grandchildren. His life has been one of goodness and grace, considering his challenges began long before the war when he was orphaned at birth.

I've had a few years now to reflect on Tom's story—and on my own misguided political past. Surprising how much I've changed. More surprising to me are those who never changed, who still cling to the illusion of their own heroic posing. My prayer is that they'll no longer be able to ignore the courage and self-sacrifice we've seen so up close and personally in the recent conflict—that they will find themselves, like me, reconsidering what is brave, what is heroic, and what will stand the test of time.

May we be truly grateful for our modern fighting corps, as well as for men like Tom Mooney. Their patriotic and unflinching service insured my freedom, though that freedom took many a strange turn before I gained the maturity to thank them for it.

Liberty Bell

★ ★ ★

That old bell now is silent,
And hushed its iron tongue,
But the spirit it awakened
Still lives—forever young.
And, while we greet the sunlight,
On the fourth of each July,
We'll ne'er forget the bellman
Who, 'twixt the earth and sky,
Rung out, loudly, "Independence!"
Which, please God, shall never die.

AUTHOR UNKNOWN

STICKERS FOR IRAQ

★★★

LYNNE M. THOMPSON

Nothing can stand in the way of God's purpose, not time, or distance, or impossible odds. And nothing can convince Tracy Scott otherwise.

For years, Tracy had wanted to contact a fondly remembered friend, Holly Higgins. But after several failed attempts at locating this classmate, Tracy gave up. Eighteen years later, she walked over to greet a visitor at her weekly women's Bible study and nearly fainted when it turned out to be Holly.

The two pals reminisced and caught up on the details of their lives, picking up their closeness right where they left off, as only old friends can do. Tracy had been serving in the United States Navy for the past fifteen years. Holly had worked in the business world and was now involved in full-time ministry. They chatted long after the meeting was over, but there was no way either of them could have foreseen the outcome of this divinely appointed meeting. Holly went home giddy over the exciting turn of events and couldn't wait to share the news with her mother, who also remembered Tracy.

Since the tragic events of September 11, 2001, Holly's ministry had been distributing stickers of the American flag affixed to a card citing

Psalm 91. In recent months, Holly's organization had attempted to contact military chaplains in order to send these cards over to troops in the Middle East, unfortunately without success.

The following week, Holly was on her way out the door to attend the Bible study when her mother called.

"You should ask that friend of yours if she knows who to talk to regarding the stickers," she suggested.

"That's a good idea," Holly said.

After the Bible study, Holly approached Tracy with her dilemma. "Would you know where I could find someone who could get us in touch with a military chaplain?" Holly asked.

Tracy smiled. "I think I can help." It just so happened that she was a chaplain's assistant with the navy reserves. And later that week she would be attending a ministries workshop in New Orleans, Louisiana, with one hundred other military chaplains and assistants from all over the United States.

Tracy took some stickers with her to the conference and found Holly the connections she needed. One month later, more than two hundred thousand stickers were on their way to U.S. troops in Kuwait and Iraq.

It was also during that conference that Tracy received orders to report to Camp Pendleton for active duty. It would be difficult to leave behind her husband, David, thirteen-year-old daughter, Amanda, and eight-year-old son, Dylan. But she wouldn't worry. God was at work.

Besides, the name of her friend's ministry is A Certain Place, and after watching God orchestrate these events, Tracy knew she was in the right one.

MY NAME IS OLD GLORY

★★★

HOWARD SCHNAUBER

I am the flag of the United States of America.
My name is Old Glory.
I fly atop the world's tallest buildings.
I stand watch in America's halls of justice.
I fly majestically over great institutes of learning.
I stand guard with the greatest military power in the world.
Look up! And see me!
I have fought every battle of every war for more than 200 years:
Gettysburg, Shiloh, Appomattox, San Juan Hill, the trenches of France,
the Argonne Forest, Anzio, Rome, the beaches of Normandy,
the deserts of Africa, the cane fields of the Philippines, the rice paddies
and jungles of Guam, Okinawa, Japan, Korea, Vietnam, Guadalcanal,
New Britain, Peleliu, and many more islands.
And a score of places long forgotten by all but those who were with me.
I was there.
I led my soldiers—I followed them.
I watched over them.
They loved me.
I was on a small hill in Iwo Jima.
I was dirty, battle-worn and tired, but my soldiers cheered me,
and I was proud.

31

I have slipped the bonds of Earth and stand watch over the
uncharted new frontiers of space
from my vantage point on the moon.
I have been a silent witness to all of America's finest hours.
But my finest hour comes when I am torn into strips to
be used for bandages for my wounded comrades on the field of battle,
When I fly at half mast to honor my soldiers,
And when I lie in the trembling arms of a grieving
mother at the graveside of her fallen son.
I am proud.
My name is Old Glory.
Dear God—long may I wave.

MUSINGS OF A
GRATEFUL CIVILIAN

DAVE MEURER

I am lying in a bed that is not my own, in a room cluttered with the debris of someone else's childhood. Boy Scouts memorabilia. T-shirts. An entire collection of Teenage Mutant Ninja Turtles on the top shelf of the closet.

I am away from home on business, overnighting at the home of a friend instead of the Holiday Inn. The room with toys is vacant because the child is gone. The closet door was already open when I entered the room. I wasn't nosing about. But I can't stop gazing into the closet. It has sucked me into a time warp.

A mere decade ago my boys used to play in this room, in this house, on this quiet street. They played with the boy who owned the ugly Mutant Turtle action figures. Dayne owned the toys. Dayne wore the Boy Scouts uniform. Dayne plastered the bunk bed with stickers.

I can see him still as I stare at his toys. Blond, skinny kid with a ready laugh. How on earth can it be that Dayne—this little boy whose bed I am borrowing for the night—has been whisked away and transformed into a soldier? Does the army have any clue that he still has all his toys stashed away? Does the Pentagon realize they have handed a machine gun to a kid?

I blink. I shake my head. I remind myself that Dayne is not a kid anymore. I moved away, and he grew up. He became an Eagle Scout.

When he graduated from high school, he told his parents he was going to join the army and protect his country.

His mom and dad, Becky and Scott, were torn between pride and fear. His dad asked Dayne if he had really stopped to think through the decision.

Dayne replied, "Dad, this country has given me so much. I have to do this."

Later, recalling the conversation, Scott looked at me—blinking back tears—and said, "How could I possibly say anything against that?"

On September 11, 2001, Dayne saw the twin towers go down. Everything changed.

Boot camp was awful, as it always is for everyone. But Dayne hung in there. He did well. His aim was so true that they cancelled his last session of target practice and let him call home while the other recruits learned to handle a weapon. Dayne has hunted his entire life. He has a leg up.

In the group photo of young, stern soldiers looking at the camera, one face stands out. It is Dayne, the only guy smiling from ear to ear. His sergeant dubs him "Sunshine." It is a ribbing, but not an insult. Dayne is irrepressibly happy about his chance to protect the folks back home. Folks like me. Middle-aged, balding, out of shape.

Dayne wanted to do something important, gutsy, and right in the face of the enemy. So he found himself on a helicopter in Iraq, doing his part to topple the mad regime of Saddam Hussein.

I am proud of this little boy who has grown into an awesome young man. I support his ongoing mission. I support his commander in chief. I pray for their success. I also pray that Dayne can come home someday, get married, and have sons who can play with the Mutant Turtle toys. (His future daughters deserve some normal dolls.)

In any war, some of our boys—only God knows the number—will not come home. I know that. Dayne's parents know that. It is a fact of war. But the alternative is letting the madmen, dictators, suicide bombers, and sociopaths dominate the world—which isn't acceptable. So, fearful and yet proud, Scott and Becky bid their son Godspeed and sent him off to war.

As I drifted off to sleep in Dayne's bed, I prayed for the boy-turned-soldier. Praying is the least I can do. And it is the most I can do.

HONORABLE DISCHARGE

JOHN SEITHER, USMC

N o one understands.

This is how I felt after arriving back in the United States from Korea, having ended my time in service and returned to civilian life. I was quite unprepared for the culture shock that awaited me. Less than two months earlier, I had been on my second tour of duty overseas. The Marine Corps had been my life for four years.

I got a job as a laborer. The late summer sun scorched my stooped body as sweat stung my eyes. I labored over the tedious task of landscape work. With every little plant that I put into the ground, I kept wondering if my military service had been worth it. I returned to the same little corner of the world that I had left only to find my peers graduating from college, well established in their careers or starting families.

Who cared that I was an expert rifleman and could put a bullet in the black from five hundred meters ten out of ten times? That is not something that one usually puts on a résumé. The fact that I could disassemble and reassemble four different machine guns and a grenade launcher with a gas mask on in the dark was meaningless. Part of my training was sending and receiving encrypted radio messages, something that had required a secret clearance. Everything I had learned meant nothing.

My buddies and I had gone to places and seen things that most people could not even imagine. The hardships we endured were just a way of life. Sometimes we slept out in the rain, other times we barely slept at all. Traveling on board ship, our racks were stacked four high. I learned to go to sleep with sweat running off my body from the constant ninety-five-degree heat and the intense humidity. I would have gladly preferred living like that again instead of the bewildering uselessness I now felt as I looked at the half-planted hill and the wheelbarrow full of seedlings.

Casualties don't always happen in wartime circumstances. A whole chopper full of marines plowed into the side of a mountain while we were in Korea, killing everyone on board. A suicide bomber killed 241 marines in Beirut. The worst for me was watching as a fellow marine was crushed between two armored vehicles. He left behind a wife and three children.

In Korea we did a large-scale exercise every year called Team Spirit. It was a live-fire maneuver with real bullets, bombs, and other ammunition used in battle. It was a very intense couple of weeks in bone-chilling weather. The South Koreans allowed us to freely operate in their towns and on their roads with all our armored vehicles and tanks. The threat from North Korea was so real, that while some countries clashed with our presence, the South Koreans gladly accepted us.

One evening, as we set up our perimeter for that night, some Korean children from a nearby town came through our position. They were a delight to interact with, although we couldn't converse. As it began to grow dark, they headed for their homes, only this time taking a direction different from the one they had used earlier. We had booby-trapped the avenue through which they made their exit. When we realized they were heading straight for the traps, it was too late. We held our breath as we watched an eight-year-old boy hit a trip wire. He stumbled briefly and then the whole group panicked and bolted. A few seconds later a harm-less flash-bang went off like a firecracker. We could hear the nervous laughter as they continued running toward their homes.

What I found to be so sad was that those kids *knew* about trip wires and booby traps. Throughout their childhood they live with the constant fear of war. I began to see that I had indeed made a significant sacrifice for my country. It was a noble thing to do. I felt proud to have been a small part of the reason American kids do not have to live with such fears.

By the grace of God, America has a force of committed men and women. We train hard, we sweat, and we bleed in peacetime and in war. To be skilled in battle is a necessity, but to serve our country is an honor. Thank God for the young men and women who sacrifice to achieve such skill. I was one of them and not ashamed. As I gathered up my tools for the evening, I looked down at the USMC tattooed on my left arm, now dirty from the day's work. I had no regrets. The mindset that my experience in the Marine Corps gave me made it all worthwhile.

Today I have my own business. When filling out documents, I look for the space provided where I can write "USMC—1980–1984, Honorable Discharge."

WITH ALL
MY HEART

JEANNIE S. WILLIAMS

Our local public school children joined with more than fifty-two million students nationwide to salute our flag and recite the Pledge of Allegiance on October 12, 2001. I asked these students if they knew the meaning of the words they were saying, and they assured me they did! I asked each of them to share with the class what the words meant to them. Afterwards, I marveled at the precious creative gifts our children possess, especially when one child added the words, "from the bottom of my heart" while reciting the pledge.

Children have an uncanny ability to lift our spirits when we least expect it. I am convinced that they are the ideal messengers for the true spirit of peace and patriotism in America. These are some of my favorite quotes from children.

I...

The first word in the Pledge of Allegiance is "I" and it means "me," one person. I was in a good place when I heard the sad news about the attack on America. I was sitting on my daddy's lap.

38

PLEDGE ALLEGIANCE...

Some people don't understand what this next part in the pledge really means. They just mouth the words. *Pledge allegiance* means that you promise from the bottom of your heart to love and protect our country. That is what our soldiers do. Some of them loved and protected our country so much they died for it.

TO THE FLAG...

This part of the pledge means you need to show your support for the American flag. Get it out and fly it. We got a new one at Wal-Mart and gave our old one to my Uncle Mike because he did not have one to fly. I am sure that he will never forget our kindness.

OF THE UNITED STATES OF AMERICA...

Of The United States of America is a bunch of territories in America that stuck together to fight the big one—World War 11. And my grandpapa says we can do it again if we have to.

AND TO THE REPUBLIC...

Republics are not democrats. My grandpa is one. But not my dad. I do not know about my grandma and my mom. They have never mentioned it to me.

FOR WHICH IT STANDS...

Me and my family went to Washington, D.C., last summer on our vacation. One day we went to the Vietnam Wall to look for my uncle's name. When we found it, my dad cried. My uncle was my dad's only brother. I was named after him. This makes me feel really proud. My Uncle Thomas was one of the brave men for which it stands.

ONE NATION UNDER GOD...

This means a land that is filled with praying people. This is a true fact because President Bush always says, "God bless America" right after he speaks to the nation. Amen.

INDIVISIBLE...

Indivisible means "that which cannot be separated or divided." I looked it up in the dictionary so I could explain it to you.

WITH LIBERTY AND JUSTICE...

Liberty is an awesome word. It means freedom.

Justice means to be kind and fair and obey the Golden Rule. To learn more about it read your Bible. Page 968.

FOR ALL...

Means everybody is included. It don't make any difference where your family lived before they came to America. Like me, for example—I lived in Kentucky before I moved to Missouri and I am half Mexican, half Indian, half Democrat, and half Baptist. But none of that makes any difference because I am an American and I always pledge allegiance to the flag of the United States of America from the bottom of my heart...

~

Our flag has never waved over
any community but in blessing.

WILLIAM MCKINLEY

DEDICATION
AND
COURAGE

★ ★ ★

GOING FORWARD

We do not retreat.
We are not content to stand still.
As Americans, we go forward,
in the service of our country,
by the will of God.

President Franklin D. Roosevelt

TOGETHER IS BETTER

★★★

STU WEBER, U.S. ARMY GREEN BERET CAPTAIN (RETIRED)
FROM ALL THE KING'S MEN

How far did we run that day? I'll never know. After so many hills, after so many miles, after so many turns through scrub brush and stands of scrawny pine, we became mindless running machines, lifting one foot after another after another after another.

All started well enough. The cadence was right. We were young. We were strong. We were soldiers. It was even exhilarating in a funny kind of way. The troops moved well. We found our rhythm. But the sun flamed ever higher in a brassy sky, the packs bit into our shoulders, our rifles grew heavier by the mile, and the dirt trail stretched endlessly on.

We'd been running every day, but this was something else. We'd been sweating from the time we rolled out of the rack before daybreak, but now moisture drained from every pore in our bodies. Sure, this was the physical training stage of U.S. Army Ranger school, and we expected exertion. Even exhaustion. But this was no morning PT rah-rah run in T-shirts.

This was something out of a nightmare.

We ran in full field uniform. Loaded packs. Helmets. Boots. Rifles. The works. As usual, the word was "You go out together, you stick together, you work as a unit, and you come in together. If you don't come in together, don't bother to come in!"

For a boy from the apple country of Washington state, the south Georgia heat felt like a soggy wool poncho draped over the top of my fatigues. The sun seared down on our helmets, burned into the metal on our nearly obsolete M-14s, drove hot needles in the exposed skin at the back of our necks. We ran through rolling country, kicking up clouds of powdery dust that stung our eyes and coated our throats.

Somewhere along the way, through a fog of pain, thirst, and fatigue, my brain registered something strange about our formation. Two rows ahead of me, I noticed one of the guys out of sync. A big, rawboned redhead named Sanderson. His legs were pumping, but he was out of step with the rest of us. Then his head began to loll from side to side. This guy was struggling. Close to losing it. Had anyone else noticed?

Yes, someone had.

Without missing a step, the ranger on Sanderson's right reached over and took the distressed man's rifle. Now one of the rangers was packing two weapons. His own and Sanderson's. The big redhead did better for awhile. The platoon kept moving, jaws slack, eyes glazed, legs pushing like pistons. But then the head began to sway again.

This time, the ranger on the left reached over, removed Sanderson's helmet, tucked it under his own arm, and continued to run. All systems go. Our boots thudded along the dirt trail in heavy unison. Tromp-tromp-tromp-tromp-tromp-tromp.

Sanderson was hurting. Really hurting. He was buckling, going down. But no. Two soldiers behind him lifted the pack off his back, each taking a shoulder strap in his free hand. Sanderson gathered his remaining strength. Squared his shoulders. And the platoon continued to run. All the way to the finish line.

We left together. We returned together. And all of us were the stronger for it.

Together is better.

GOODBYE

★ ★ ★

L. REBECA DEBOARD

We sat on wet grass in front of concrete barracks, lifting our faces to warm sunshine and a cool breeze, fighting the cold grasping fingers of an eerie silence. All of the words had been said, all of the tears had been shed. The day had come to send my brother-in-law, Sergeant Randall Ricketts, to war. *Sacrifice. Duty. Honor.* They were all about to become part of our lives.

Having fought in Desert Storm, Randall knew exactly what he would endure. His face was set in stone, the only outward picture of an inner storm was the rapid pulse at his neck. I wondered if my sister noticed. She stood under the oak tree, twisting the diamond band Randall had placed on her finger nearly ten years ago. Her turns matched the time of his pulse.

"Aunt Boo, when will Daddy be back?" My towheaded niece plopped down in the grass beside me.

"We're not sure, sweetie," I answered and held her close.

"He has to go make sure that mean man doesn't hurt us?" Her small voice carried across the yard to the other children. They looked up, waiting for my answer.

"That's right, Katie. Sometimes people are really mean. When that happens, the nice people have to help. That's what Daddy's going to do.

He wants to make sure that mean man doesn't hurt us." We had been over this before. I watched the other children go back to making circles in the dirt with broken sticks. They had obviously been over it, too.

"It's seventeen forty-eight!" my nephew announced after stealing a glance at his daddy's watch. Formation was scheduled for eighteen hundred. Alex had been counting down since seventeen thirty-three, not realizing the effect of his words. We all began making our way to the back courtyard to prepare for formation.

Stepping into brighter sunshine on the west side of the building, my eyes protested the bright glare. All around me, those in uniform were hugging, crying, comforting the ones to be left behind. I looked at my sister. No tears yet. *Sacrifice.*

"It's seventeen fifty-three!" Alex announced. Seven minutes stretched out as an eternity. Alex and Katie stole away to a playground about a hundred yards away, escaping the thick wall of tension surrounding the adults.

More silent minutes ticked by.

"Where are Katie and Alex?" My sister broke from her daze long enough to realize the kids were nowhere in sight.

"Probably at the playground," I said. "I'll go get them." I began weaving my way through tight knots of family clusters, some praying, most weeping. Locating my niece and nephew, I knelt down in front of them.

"Listen, Mommy and Daddy are pretty upset because Daddy is leaving. How about we go love on them and make them feel better?" Having been dragged back to the tension-filled world of adults, the kids hung their heads and took my hand. We rejoined the family. *Duty.*

Alex grabbed his daddy's wrist and stole another glance at the military watch.

"It's seventeen fifty-nine!"

"Son, that's enough." Randall's patience had worn thin. "Do not look at my watch again." My sister's look let me know what his words confirmed, the inner turmoil was being held beneath a facade growing weak. I held my breath as nearly two hundred soldiers began lining up in formation. *Honor.*

"Soldiers, we've got a job to do." Captain Turner's words had their desired effect. I watched each soldier's chin come up just a notch.

"Everyone knows why we're here. Let's go get it done. Load up." *Sacrifice. Duty. Honor.*

Every soldier rushed to a family member. These were the last hugs for at least a year. Randall put his big arms around Alex's little body. "Love you, Bud."

"Love you, Buddy." Alex turned his face to the ground.

Randall turned to me, with Katie up on my shoulders. I held my brother-in-law and felt the rough fabric of his uniform against my cheek. "I love you." Words not spoken often between us. Katie kissed the top of his head from her perch on my shoulders. "Love you, Daddy."

"Love you, Baby Girl."

I turned to see my precious sister's face. Her beautiful brown eyes full of love and tears, locked onto Randall's face. He held her, a protective and tender embrace, then slung his bag over a shoulder and turned to the bus. We all stood there, frozen, watching his back. Was this really happening?

"Let's walk over to the buses," I said. "Come on, maybe we can figure out which one he's on."

We all began walking beside the buses, peering into small windows. He was in the second-to-last bus. Christie walked over to his window. I knew they were talking, but couldn't hear above the calls of others to their loved ones. Realization dawned, though, when she turned from the bus to walk back to us. Her face now dissolved into tears. Words not spoken often between them.

"Why is Momma crying?" Katie asked. I picked her up and put my nose to hers.

"Because she's sad, sweet girl."

"'Cause Daddy's leaving?" she twirled my hair in her hand.

"Yes, sweetie, because Daddy is leaving and we miss him already."

The bus engines started to rev, silencing the crowd. As the big tires slowly began to roll, a lady began clapping.

"Go get 'em, ya'll!" she hollered and punched a fist in the air. The crowd joined in her support. Waves of applause rippled through the crowd, joined by whistles and cheers. All five buses lumbered away, leaving in their wake a crying, cheering, aching crowd. *Sacrifice. Duty. Honor.* The countdown had begun.

ON MISSION

✯✯✯

CHUCK HOLTON
FORMER U.S. ARMY RANGER
ADAPTED FROM *A MORE ELITE SOLDIER*

I'm aroused from deep thought by the shout of the jumpmaster over the roar of aircraft engines. It's almost 1 A.M. on December 20, 1989. I'm one of nearly one hundred Airborne Rangers who, four hours ago at Fort Benning, Georgia, packed onto this C-130 transport that was built for sixty-four jumpers. I carry the rank of specialist, E4.

"Outboard personnel, stand UP!"

I look across at my friend Philip Lear, and he gives me a wry smile. Earlier this year, Lear and I were assigned as buddies in Ranger school, a two-month leadership course where we were allowed one meal a day and two hours of sleep a night, if we were lucky.

We've been through a lot together. It was by pure chance that we ended up on this plane together. This is the first we've seen of each other since the day we graduated Ranger school ten months ago. I regret that we haven't been able to do much catching up on the ride down; a C-130 aircraft is incredibly noisy. He did tell me that he has gotten engaged. Once we hit the ground we must go our separate ways, as his platoon has a different job to do.

"Inboard personnel, stand UP!"

I can't believe it's gone this far. We may actually do this mission.

We've been called up for real life missions before, but they've always been cancelled at the last minute. This time our destination is Panama. The overall mission is to take down their corrupt dictator, Manuel Noriega, and establish a democratic government. It's nice to think that the army might finally use us. We've been training for this mission for months.

"Hook up!"

We all struggle to attach our static lines to the overhead cable that will pull our chutes open once we exit the aircraft. The task is made difficult by the fact that we can hardly move. I wonder if our leaders planned it this way so that we will be anxious to jump. If they did, it's working. I am careful to ensure that my static line is securely fastened to the cable, though my faith in getting to the ground safely does not lie in the cable above me or the parachute on my back. If it did, I don't know that I would have ever made it through jump school to begin with.

"Check equipment!"

We do our best to check each other out in the dim light of the aircraft interior. I try to ensure that there's nothing under my feet that I might trip on heading for the door. I can't see my feet. My heart starts beating faster.

"Sound off for equipment check!"

Someone slaps me on the shoulder. I tap the guy in front of me and shout "Okay!" He taps the guy in front of him, and so on, toward the jumpmaster at the rear of the aircraft. Once the jumpmaster gets the "All okay" signal, he will open the aircraft door and begin spotting for the drop zone.

The white lights go out. To say that it's uncomfortable standing with an eighty-pound rucksack full of ammunition hanging between your legs is a severe understatement. My M-203 grenade launcher is in its case strapped securely on my left side.

Suddenly, I hear the roar of the night outside as the doors open at the rear of the aircraft. I can just see the red light next to the door that will soon turn green, telling us when to jump. The jumpmaster takes hold of the doorframe and leans far out of the aircraft, looking for the airfield. All he sees is water. When we jump, there won't even be time to pull my reserve parachute if my main doesn't open. I'm not sure why I even wore one except that it is simply a force of habit.

I feel a quiet sense of peace. This is where I'm supposed to be at this moment, and I believe that if one seeks to follow God's purpose for his life, there's no safer place to be. Besides, we're armed to the teeth and we've got a job to do.

I happen to glance toward the window just in time to see two closely spaced flashes of light. There's no going back now. There are two stealth fighter aircraft flying with us that dropped two 2000-pound bombs on the leading edge of the airfield to kick off the invasion.

A testosterone-filled "HOOAH!" goes up from the rangers in our aircraft.

"Drop zone coming up!" the jumpmaster screams. I can't hear him, but I see his lips moving and know what he's saying. Lear reaches over and slaps me on the helmet.

The light goes green. Rangers start shuffling out the door. The C-130 starts banking sharply left, then right. The pilots are taking evasive action to avoid antiaircraft fire. Now I really want out of this plane. Everything around me moves in blurry slow motion, but my consciousness is razor sharp.

Ten feet from the door, the light turns red, signaling the end of the drop zone. The Air Force loadmaster steps up and tries to get us to stop jumping. Everyone ignores him. There's no way we're not jumping now. I run for the door and step into blackness…

I'm on mission.

HOG WILD

★★★

MIKE PARKER

I t is *amazing how peaceful life could be at 20,000 feet,* the rugged young
airman thought above the drone of the four 2200 horsepower
engines. Seated behind the 50-caliber automatic at the waist gunner position of a B-29 Superfortress affectionately dubbed *The Hog Wild,* thoughts
of his wife and one-month old son flitted across his mind, and a smile
creased his face. Then his world exploded. Caught in the searchlights of a
North Korean antiaircraft battery, *The Hog Wild* was blown apart.

When he regained his senses, Fred Parker, Jr. found himself outside
the fuselage, being dragged by his feet through the night air. He kicked
free, and as he was taught by the air force, tucked into a tight body position and pulled the ripcord of his emergency parachute. Miraculously, a
sea of white silk opened above him and he floated to the ground, just
short of the Yaloo River.

Evade and escape. Fred had undergone the rigorous, some would say
brutal, Air Force Survival School in Colorado. On September 13, 1952, he
was glad for the training. "I was free eleven days from the day I went down
until I was captured," Fred remembers. "It took another month before I
reached a permanent POW camp. During that time I didn't see another
American. Looking back I am proud of the fact that I never lost my cool

during that whole experience. My mind was clear. I did the things I was trained to do and it saved my life."

Fred remained a prisoner of war for thirteen months. He was released during the prisoner exchange known as Operation Big Switch. It was only then that his young wife learned that he was still alive; the sole surviving member of the eleven-man crew of the ill-fated B-29.

When asked why she never gave up hope, she replied simply, "He told me he would come back and he has never lied to me."

Although offered an immediate discharge, Fred elected to remain in the air force to fulfill his obligation. Why? "Commitment is the word that comes to mind," Fred answers without hesitation. "When you give your word, when you make a commitment to your country, to your job, to your wife, to God—you should stick with it through good times and bad times."

More than just a word, commitment is a way of life for Fred. After completing his commitment to Uncle Sam, Fred committed thirty years to a single company before retiring from IBM. And he recently celebrated his marriage commitment by celebrating his fifty-second wedding anniversary.

"Commitment," Fred insists, "is the thread that ties it all together."

~

God grant that men of principle
shall be our principal men.

THOMAS JEFFERSON

THE SOLDIERS
OF BATAAN

PHILIP S. BRAIN, JR.

*Davao Penal Colony, a rice farm in the middle of the Philippine jungles,
was home to a thousand American prisoners of war
who survived the Bataan Death March.
With the constant horrors of malaria, low rations,
and sixteen-hour work details, how did these men keep their faith?*

The rain thundered on the tin roof of my prison camp barracks; for twelve long hours there had been no letup. I lay shivering on my hard, wooden bunk, pulling a threadbare blanket around me. My fellow prisoners had been working in the rice fields since six that morning. I felt guilty as I glanced at the empty beds surrounding me, but I'd just been released from the prison hospital. Otherwise I, too, would have been working for hours in the wind and rain, standing in ankle-deep mud, clad only in a loincloth.

With my hands stiff from the damp chill, I smoothed the crumpled note that had been smuggled to me the night before. "Phil, I've just been operated on again. More bone off the leg. Would like to see you if you feel like coming. Walt."

Lord, what should I do, what can I say? I prayed, for I knew that Walt and the other men in the hospital were in danger. Our fellow prisoners were plotting to take over the camp. Some Filipino guerrilla soldiers, eager to fight back at the Japanese any way they could, had made contact with some of us as we worked in the rice fields. "We'll help you overthrow your captors," the guerrillas promised, "and you can hide with us in the jungle." The Japanese didn't guard us in the fields. Instead, they made us toil without clothing or food, reasoning that we couldn't escape then. But with the help of the guerrillas....

Only one thing had delayed the plan. If anyone escaped, the guards would kill the sick or wounded instantly. Even if we somehow protected them, we still wouldn't be able to carry all of them safely into the jungle. So we kept planning, hoping to find a way without sacrificing anyone. *Lord, we may all die if we stay here much longer, but how can we escape without bringing every man along? What should we do?*

I read the note once more. Walt and I had been in the prison hospital when I was recovering from malaria. The "hospital" was a nearby hut where men too sick to stand lay on damp, sagging cots. On one of my first days, I heard someone singing a Theta Delta Chi fraternity song. In the fog of fever, I turned toward the cot right next to me. My mind shot back to America, college, and the loyal friends I'd known. Homesickness washed over me, yet I felt suddenly comforted by the presence of a fraternity brother.

"I was Theta Delta Chi at Minnesota," I said weakly. "Name's Phil."

"Walt, Michigan," he answered. "Small world and all that."

To pass the time, we tried to top each other's fraternity pranks—anything to forget where we were. Walt admitted, "We stole the clapper from the bell tower right before graduation. They couldn't toll the bells to start the ceremony!"

I laughed, yet I could see the stained bandages engulfing the lower part of Walt's leg. They had amputated his foot. And he was still singing.

A few days passed. Walt continued to receive treatment for his leg, but I got out of the hospital as soon as I could. Sick prisoners were given only half rations.

Now, staring at Walt's note, I knew that if I wanted to see him, I'd have to sneak back into the hospital that night. "Walt needs a friend," I told myself.

Again, I prayed. *Lord, what are we to do?* My prayers turned circles in my head. No outcome seemed right.

Around nine that night, I left the shelter of my barracks to see Walt. A dim light from the nearby mess shack lit my way. Between the low-hanging clouds and heavy sheets of rain, the Japanese guards couldn't see me creeping about.

The other prisoners were still out in the fields. Perhaps the Japanese knew something was afoot. Perhaps they'd increased our hours in the fields, hoping someone would crack and betray the plot.

With conditions so terrible, I wondered if some of the men might act on their own. I'd spent months in those fields with four hundred men—hungry, sick, and driven by bayonets to work. An escape might happen tonight.

I slipped into the hospital. Most of the men were asleep. I didn't have the heart to tell Walt about the plot. "Walt," I whispered, "the light was still on in the mess shack. The men assigned to the rice detail today are still out in the rice fields."

Weak as he was, Walt sparked with anger. "First they take away our food, water, and shoes so we won't escape out there. Then they work us worse than mules. But—" he grimaced with pain—"they can't break us."

We chatted a bit more, exchanging news about some of the other prisoners. Walt and I shook hands before I left. I wondered if I'd ever see him again.

I crept back toward the barracks. As I neared the mess hall, I heard a sound above the rain. I listened. My heart stopped beating for a second and then raced as it never had before. I realized I was hearing the diesel engine that pulled the flatcars the men rode back from the rice fields. But it was the sound of men yelling that had made my heart race.

I was sure the prisoners on detail had overpowered the guards and were taking over the camp. *Lord, it's over. Be with Walt and all the others,* I prayed as I tried to decide which direction to run.

The light flashed on in the house of the Japanese commander as he ran out on the porch to investigate the commotion.

The train stopped about a hundred yards from the main gate. I could just barely see the shapes of men piling off, shouting even louder. I strained to listen with every bit of me, and the noise began to take form. Soon, tears mingled with the rain on my face. The men weren't shouting. They were *singing*. As they lined up in columns of four to march into the compound, the words of "God Bless America" floated through the air: "...through the night with the light from above...."

I relaxed and joined in the cheering as the men came through the barbed-wire gates. No one was going to escape; we were sticking together, a profound example of the brotherhood our country stood for. Walt wouldn't die tonight, and neither would I.

The next morning, the Japanese commander ordered all prisoners to line up. He then went up to the American commanding officer, saluted, and said, "I honor the spirit of the soldiers of Bataan." He pointed to the gate, where some of his men were bringing in wheelbarrows full of avocados and bananas and other tropical fruit. As we stood, waiting for our portion of his gift, I thought, *Walt was right, they couldn't break us, not with our faith in God and faith in America.* From that moment, I began believing I might live.

Even now, at the age of eighty-seven, the strains of "God Bless America" bring me to tears. I've never stopped talking to the God who stands beside us even in the darkest of times.

Editor's note: Walt also survived the war, and the two soldiers corresponded until Walt's death in the 1990s.

PRESERVING MEMORIES

★ ★ ★

BETTY KING

B uck was one of those good old boys.

He stopped in every morning along with a few other regulars at mom and pop's restaurant over on the south end of town. They never ate breakfast. They were coffee drinkers. They could drink several pots for the price of a cup. Nobody objected, least of all me. I was the hostess. My mother-in-law and husband owned and operated the smorgasbord. I saw past the coffee drinkers need for the hot simmering caffeine and simply listened when they talked. I enjoyed their company; they reminded me of Dad.

Soon, Buck and a few of the other boys were dropping by two and three times during the day. Buck even brought in fish he'd caught and the cooks offered their services. Buck's perch, mom and pop's hush puppies, coleslaw, and fried potatoes made good excuses for gathering conversations. My husband liked Buck too, and Buck's wife enjoyed the fish fries.

"Were you in the war, Buck?"

"Yeah."

"Where'd you serve at; what company, Buck? Tell me about it."

Buck was reluctant to reveal his part in conquering Omaha Beach, but I had a way of pulling memories from him—some things lay hidden too long. I encouraged, praised, and was in awe of the tanks he had guided through the villages. He told me about bullets that had gone through his helmet, and about the fear that had gripped him. Stories he'd never told rushed forth. I listened.

"Have you ever told these stories to your wife and kids, Buck?"

"Nope."

"Why not?"

"'Cause. They wouldn't be interested. It wasn't noth'n."

"Oh yes, they would! Trust me. They would."

As days passed, I encouraged Buck to share with me all the things he had buried. I heard stories straight from the battlefields. A brave young soldier emerged from behind steaming coffee cups. I began to see blurry paintings of the young man behind the years—years before the construction worker, years before retirement, and years before a Cold War. I saw a young man who left behind his sweetheart and faced the waves that took many a young soldier before he ever reached the sandy beach. I saw a man who dodged bullets and saw enemies face-to-face. I got glimpses of a weary man who saw his buddies fall and left them on bloody battlefields. Dried tears glistened from the eyes of an old warrior who was fortunate to return home.

I knew it. He knew it. Others should know it.

"Buck, let me videotape you. Let me just talk with you. You can tell me all of these things, and then give it as a gift to your children. It would mean so much to them."

"No, I couldn't do that."

"Just think about it, Buck. It would be a wonderful gift straight from your heart."

Buck enjoyed his talks with me. He caught hold of every chance he got to speak to my attentive ears. When business became slow, I listened longer. I began to see his chest swell with pride for the things I admired about him. He sought from me more than admiration and validation. I was someone he could bounce his memories off of.

"I've been thinking about what you suggested. Maybe I could do that. Perhaps they would like to hear about my part in the war after all."

We never got around to the videotape. Some things get left on a shelf and put off for too long. Then one day Buck's wife called; she wanted me to know that Buck was gone. Often in life, death comes too suddenly.

I suddenly wished we had not put off the videotaping. I did, though, share with his family those things that had filled his heart. That far away look he often held in his eyes was hard to convey, but I will never forget it.

As I sit now watching a new kind of war, one we can view on our television screens, I think of Buck. I think of the sacrifices he made and the patriotism that swelled up from inside him. I see that same pride today in our service men and women as they serve. They are fighting to preserve my freedom and those of people across oceans, the same as Buck did. Times have changed, but those who serve are the same; they serve with pride a country they love.

I wish to thank all those who preserved my freedom and my children's freedom. I wish to thank those who continue to serve, to ensure my grandchildren and their children's children's freedom. God bless each and every one of you.

∽

Courageous isn't something you are,
it's something you do.

CHUCK HOLTON, U.S. ARMY RANGER

Renewed Strength

★ ★ ★

Even youths grow tired and weary,
and young men stumble and fall;
but those who hope in the LORD
will renew their strength.
They will soar on wings like eagles;
they will run and not grow weary,
they will walk and not be faint.

FROM THE BIBLE
ISAIAH 40:30–31

ONCE A MARINE, ALWAYS A MARINE

BIRDIE L. ETCHISON

My father, Leland Leighton, joined the marines the first time as an eighteen-year-old, bright-eyed kid. He and a friend had hitchhiked from Portland, Oregon, to Los Angeles—not an uncommon thing to do in 1936. They were penniless when picked up and listed as vagrants. Daddy said yes when a recruiter suggested he enter the corps and become a marine.

Then came 1945. World War II had been raging since 1941. My father, now married with three children, knew he would be called up any day. He decided to sign up before he got the call because he wanted to join the navy this time.

As he stood, waiting in the induction center, he heard his name called. He looked up to find a burly sergeant standing there. A marine. Daddy mumbled something about wanting the navy, but the sergeant bellowed, "Son, once a marine, always a marine."

Back to MCRD (boot camp) my father went. I was eight years old and remember crying as I stood, clutching the trembling hand of my mother, as the train pulled out of the station.

But God was merciful, because the war came to an end the day before my father was to ship overseas. In November 1945, he came back home.

Tears of joy now cascaded down our cheeks when we picked him up from the train station.

Skipping ahead several decades to 2003, my father, no longer his robust, healthy self, entered a hospice facility. His time had come. He died the night of April 7.

In Yuma, Arizona, his great-granddaughter, Samantha, a marine corporal, recently married to her marine corporal boyfriend, received the news about Grandpa. Could they possibly come to Oregon to pay respects at the services for a fallen marine?

With the help of the Red Cross, they were on their way, driving the distance in twenty hours. They came, though not in uniform, as there hadn't been time to get ready. They were there proud in heart and spirit.

Nine marines attended the memorial—all but one a family member: two nephews, three grandsons, a granddaughter, a great-granddaughter, a great-grandson, and a friend. And as I gave the eulogy for my beloved father, I closed with the "Marine Hymn," the first song I had learned at age two. My heart swelled with pride as I remember what my father had been, what he had done, and how he had been instrumental in raising seven of those marines now standing at attention at his funeral. My mother, head held high, received the American flag as taps played in the background.

It was an awesome moment for one marine called home, and for those who came to say good-bye.

FROM MY
TANK'S PERCH

TARMO HOLMA
41ST TANK BATALLION, 11TH ARMORED DIVISION
AS TOLD TO TRICIA GOYER

When World War II first broke out, I was drafted and sent to Fort Hood to be a part of the tank destroyers. Training and preparations went fine but bad news was awaiting me when I tried to board the ship leaving for the European theater. My commander said I couldn't go because I wasn't a U.S. citizen. I had come to America with my parents from Finland when I was young and I never realized I wasn't a citizen until I attempted to leave for Europe. Instead I was sent to California where I took citizenship classes and joined a new division—the 11th Armored Division. They too needed tank crew members and put me on a tank. I didn't have to walk, so I liked that position. The only problem was, I hated being cooped up, so I sat on top of the tank almost the whole way through Europe. I guess most people figured I wouldn't survive up there, but I liked it. I had a whole new view of the world.

Yes, I got quite a view from on top of that tank. As soon as we landed in France, our division was rerouted to Belgium. The Battle of the Bulge had just begun, and they needed us for support. Our armored trucks and tanks rumbled through the recently freed Paris, and all the girls came out to greet us. It was a big event. I can still see it, our tanks rolling through the crowds. I even got a view of the L'Arc de Triomphe. But we didn't stop to celebrate. We had work to do.

The Bulge was hard. We lost many men but finally defeated the Germans in Belgium. Our division attempted to move on to take Berlin, but instead we were sent south to Austria. We heard our president made an agreement with the Russians to allow them to capture Berlin.

On our way to Austria, there is one thing I will never forget. The image of what I spotted from my perch on that tank still brings tears to my eyes nearly sixty years later.

One day I was riding along and looking around with my binoculars, very curious. Our unit was in the advanced guard. As we crested a hill, a sight took my breath away. I radioed the operations major.

"Major," I said. "I believe the whole German Army must be down there. The road is full of people. Just a black line."

I couldn't distinguish what kind of people they were, but I could see that black line stretched out for miles.

I said again, "The whole German Army must be down there waiting for us."

He answered very quietly. "No, son, that's the prisoners from Flossenberg concentration camp. The Germans wanted to clear them out before we got there."

As I looked at that mass of people, I wish I'd known about this before. The Germans had emptied the camps and were attempting to march the prisoners further into the interior. The prisoners reminded me of walking skeletons. And as our tanks rolled past the columns we were told not to offer them food. The prisoner's bodies were no longer used to food, and it would kill them. It was hard moving on, not being able to help. But our commanders promised the medics coming behind would care for the prisoners.

Not too many weeks after that, we rolled into Austria and soon the war ended. While in Austria, General Patton ordered all his men in the 3rd Army to visit the camps. He wanted his soldiers to see what they had been fighting for. I didn't go. I didn't need to. I'd seen enough on that roadside. Enough to stir pained memories for a lifetime.

Yes, from the top of that tank I'd seen it all—the battles, the barbarity of men, and the joy of liberation. From my perch I witnessed what I'll never forget—the fight between good and evil. And I was thankful I was part of bringing in the good.

A SOLDIER'S CHRISTMAS

★ ★ ★

CHUCK HOLTON
FROM *A MORE ELITE SOLDIER*

My head throbbed along with the engines of the massive Air Force HH-53 helicopter. I wanted to sleep; it had been a week since I'd gotten more than a couple of hours' rest at a time, but the anticipation of the mission wouldn't allow it. I noticed a spare set of headphones lying on the floor next to the crew chief, plugged into the aircraft's radio system. I donned them quickly, hoping to get some more information about our target by listening to the pilots.

It was Christmas Day, 1989, but I hardly noticed. I was serving in the U.S. Army with the 75th Ranger Regiment. Six days earlier, my unit had taken part in the invasion of Panama, the start of Operation Just Cause. What had looked like a simple operation that would have us home by Christmas had dragged on day after day, and had now become a wild goose chase for Panama's elusive dictator, Manuel Noriega. On this day, we had been sent on a mission to a small town named David on the northern end of Panama near Costa Rica to secure an airfield and search for holdout elements of the Panamanian Defense Forces, loyal to Noriega.

On the two-hour helicopter ride to David from Howard Air Force Base in the Canal Zone, I wasn't in a particularly good mood. My girlfriend and I had been planning a trip to Fort Worth, Texas, so that she could meet my parents over the Christmas holiday. Soon after I walked into the compound though, they had locked it down, shutting the Rangers in our unit off from the outside world. She knew nothing of what had happened until the news reported our invasion of this tropical country. Now it was Christmas Day and I was sweating in the belly of a cargo helicopter speeding toward what we had been told could be a protracted battle with Noriega's last loyal defenders.

Anticipation and dread rose in my stomach as I listened to the banter over the chopper's radio. A scout helicopter had flown ahead and sent back a report that there were over one thousand people on the ground, possibly hostile. This was a much greater number than expected. Being a lower ranking enlisted man meant I had not been briefed very thoroughly on what we would actually encounter once we hit the ground. It was now clearly obvious that we had lost the element of surprise. Our group of rangers numbered only 127. My prayers for protection changed to prayers for deliverance.

The missions that we had performed prior to this one had taught me something unexpected about the nature of combat. The fear was always most intense before the shooting started. Once bullets started flying, the anxiety dissolved into white-hot focused purpose. This was a dividend of the tough, realistic training that we constantly pursued in peacetime. For this reason, I was quite anxious for this helicopter ride to end. I knew that the only way to get rid of the apprehension that I was feeling was to get on mission.

The six helicopters swooped into the airfield at David and landed en masse on the tarmac. Our assault group deployed from them as quickly as possible. Each one of us was grimly aware that this might be our last Christmas. I dropped my goggles over my eyes just before charging off the tailgate of the HH-53 into the windstorm created by its massive eight-bladed rotor disk. The choppers picked up and departed as quickly as they had come, shrouding us in swirling dust.

As the dust settled, we were greeted with an incredible sight. The people on the ground weren't enemy soldiers, as we had feared, but the residents of the town, coming to greet us with banners and cheers. We had been expecting a firefight and had found ourselves in a parade. The crowd swarmed around us, excited and welcoming, as we approached the flight terminal in a wedge formation.

But our troubles weren't over. It was very possible that there were, in fact, some hostile elements in the crowd. If they engaged us in this setting, we wouldn't be able to defend ourselves without causing massive civilian casualties. The order quickly came down from our leaders—get the civilians out of here.

I was one of the few soldiers in my platoon who spoke any Spanish. Suddenly every squad leader wanted my help at once. The tropical sun beat down on my flak vest, Kevlar helmet, and rucksack full of ammo, and I soon found myself exhausted and sweating profusely as I scurried around trying to translate for people and get the locals to leave the airfield. It was a very tense few moments, trying to watch every waving hand for a grenade, staying on the lookout for any hostile movement. Finally, we got the majority of the crowd beginning to leave. My stress meter was pegged, and I was really starting to feel the effects of the heat. I needed some relief.

Suddenly, I felt an urgent tugging at the back of my pants leg. I whirled around and raised my rifle, prepared to defend myself.

At the end of my gun sight stood a beautiful little girl, maybe four years old. Her wide eyes looked up at me as she stood frozen in fear. She was barefoot and wore a cute little pink dress.

Her little hands trembled as she reached up and handed me something brought from her father, who was standing nearby.

And at that moment, in the city of David on Christmas Day, I received one of my most memorable Christmas gifts—a reminder that God knows exactly where I am and what I need, even when I don't have time to ask.

An ice-cold soda.

THE FEW, THE PROUD...

✯ ✯ ✯

Tom Neven
U.S. Marine Corps

I t's two against one. I stand in a sandpit wearing a modified football helmet and a lot of protective gear. I hold a pugil stick, a four-foot pole with pads on each end, kind of like a giant Q-Tip. Two opponents, similarly dressed and armed, face me.

It's a sweltering, late-August day in 1975 at the Marine Corps Recruit Depot on Parris Island, South Carolina. I'm a little more than midway through the thirteen weeks of sheer hell the marines call boot camp.

Quit. Quit. Quit. The thought has surfaced at least three times a day since I arrived back in early July. It's echoing around my head now. Somehow, though, I just can't. Sure, I'm worried about how *I* would look if I quit; more important, though, I don't want to let down my buddies, which is what I fear most at the moment—not the two guys just waiting to give me a severe thumping. To quit or lose would be letting down my platoon in this interplatoon pugil stick competition.

The referee's whistle blows. The instructor's advice echoes in my head: *Keep moving. Don't let them come at you two abreast.* I shuffle my feet in the soft sand, attempting to get to the side of one of my opponents as I keep my pugil stick at the ready position diagonally across my body. By my constantly moving, one opponent is always blocked by his partner, allowing me to fight them one at a time.

Blows from the other guy's stick rain down on my arms and shoulders, but none is a killer to the torso or head. I find myself possessed by an aggressiveness I didn't know I had. I shift right and lunge straight at the first guy. My pugil stick strikes pay dirt directly against the front of his helmet.

Tweeet! The whistle signals a halt to the fight as the "dead" guy is ordered out of the pit. My platoon mates let out a mighty roar. It's now one-on-one.

I'm deathly exhausted. The pugil stick feels as if it weighs two tons. My leg muscles burn from the constant jumping and lunging in soft sand.

Tweeet! The match starts again. The other guy is looking a bit worried. I'm ready to end this thing—NOW! I attack and pummel the poor guy. He puts up a fight, but I lunge forward and nail him with a thrust to the chest.

Tweeet! The referee points to the other guy and motions out of the pit with his thumb.

"Good job, recruit!" the instructor says.

I turn in exultation toward my platoon, pugil stick held in victory over my head. The guys go wild at my victory, slapping me on the back as I climb out of the protective gear. Our drill instructor, Staff Sergeant Pulley, nods approval. I get the impression he didn't think I had it in me.

Frankly, neither did I at the time. That win in the pugil stick pit was a turning point for me. After that day, I was confirmed in my mind that I was going to make it through boot camp and earn the title, U.S. Marine. Up to that point, I'd been filled with doubts. After all, the marines' recruiting slogan at the time was "We're Looking for a Few Good Men." Problem was, I didn't consider myself one of those few. I wasn't a big man on campus in high school. I didn't play football; I marched in the band.

But the rigors of marine boot camp cultivated in me a determination never to quit. Those weeks at Parris Island gave me courage to go forward no matter how scared or tired I was and gave me a self-discipline I lacked. Marine basic training was like the narrow point of a wedge that separated all that went before from what followed, and that fight was the very sharpest point of that wedge. I still wonder to this day what my life would be like if I hadn't won that pugil stick bout.

THE WINNER

✯ ✯ ✯

Martha E. Gorris

Midshipman Fred Gorris waited with the other students at the Naval Academy for the dreaded list to be posted. His white uniform was soaked with perspiration as he shifted from one leg to the other in the late May heat. Finally a yeoman came out of the office and posted the list.

Fred moaned when he saw his name. It meant he had to appear at an academic board that afternoon. He'd been on academic probation most of the year, because of math—namely, calculus and differential equations.

That afternoon he met the superintendent for the first time. "Face up to it, Mr. Gorris. You just don't have what it takes to stay here," barked the admiral. "Look, I know you went to prep school and worked hard there, but you simply can't handle the math load here at the navy. Attend a civilian college—go through OCS [Officer Candidate School]. You can still have a career in the navy. In fact, I'll see that you get a good recommendation."

The admiral stood up, indicating that the interview was over.

"Aye, aye, sir!" Fred executed a sharp about-face and left the paneled office.

He retreated to the chapel not far away. He sat in the peaceful hush and recalled the events of recent months. He'd studied hard, but the pace was merciless. He'd dreamed of the Naval Academy for as long as he could remember. Now his dream was slipping out of his grasp.

Emerging into the late afternoon sunshine, Fred's love for the Academy with all its history and tradition flooded through him. His favorite hero, John Paul Jones, was buried in the chapel. After pondering Jones's life, Fred stood straighter with a new determination. He knew what he had to do.

Walking back to Bancroft Hall, he considered that for most of his twenty-two years, people around him had been telling him all the things he *couldn't* do. He couldn't make the track team, couldn't be elected Key Club treasurer, couldn't get into the Naval Academy.

"Well, I'm tired of hearing what I can't do! I can do it and I will."

The next day, Saturday, he set the appeal process in motion. He was granted a hearing date on Monday.

He spent the day in the library preparing. As he wrote, he prayed, *Help me choose the right words, Lord.*

When Monday dawned, Fred looked his best: whites, a shined belt buckle, and spit-polished shoes. Clasping clammy hands behind his back, he paced the formal waiting room. Perspiring, somber midshipmen were seated stiffly—waiting.

The first midshipman to come back through those doors hung his head, fighting tears. No one spoke. No one needed to.

An agonizing twenty minutes later, the second young man came out, head held high, his lips pursed tightly. The mood in the room darkened.

At last the admiral's aide appeared. "Gorris!"

Fred followed the aide. *Father, help me now.*

Behind a long green table, he saw the stern faces of fifteen high-ranking officers. At the head sat the superintendent, almost regal in appearance. He leaned over, talking to the captain on his right. They laughed heartily.

The officers chatted quietly between themselves. A foul cigar burned in an ashtray, creating a smoke cloud that stung Fred's eyes.

They seemed oblivious to his entry, until the admiral opened a folder and looked directly at him. Instantly it was back to business.

"Well, Mr. Gorris, we meet again. You don't quit easily, do you?"

Obviously not expecting an answer, he continued. "Your math grades are the issue. They are sadly below acceptable standards."

Fred maintained an erect posture, fighting the urge to panic.

"However, we found your appeal to be persuasive," the admiral said. "Your quote from John Paul Jones, 'He who will not risk cannot win,' seems to indicate your resolve and character. We need men in this navy with that kind of determination. Mr. Gorris, this board has decided to grant your request for more time in study. That is, you must turn back one year, repeat your math courses, and bring them up to Academy standards.

"Therefore, this board grants your request to continue at the Naval Academy, to—in your words—'fulfill your impossible dream.' Carry on, midshipman. You're dismissed!"

"Yes, sir!" Fred executed an about-face. Outside, he let out a whoop that cut through the gloom of the waiting room.

His first stop was his domed refuge. His pounding heart quieted as he knelt in the chapel. "Thank you, Lord. I'll make it this time."

He had God's help on his side. He couldn't possibly lose.

NO MATTER
HOW TOUGH

CHUCK HOLTON

S taff Sergeant Jeff Strueker knew he was about to die.

His world was a whirlwind of chaos, a relentless tornado that he was sure would swallow him at any second. His pulse pounded in his ears over the sound of the firestorm that engulfed him. Stinging sand burned his throat, blurred his vision. If he'd had time to think about it, he might have been able to convince himself that this was all a nightmare.

But there wasn't time to think, only react. This was real.

This was Mogadishu.

One of his men lay dead. Others with him were wounded. There was enemy fire pouring in from all directions. The dark green Humvee they were riding in was a giant slow-moving target, and it carried no armor to protect his soldiers from the bullets and rocket-propelled grenades that seemed to come from every direction as they sped toward the U.S.-controlled airfield and safety.

This was not Strueker's first time in combat. In his six years as a U.S. Army Ranger, he had experienced two previous conflicts, in Panama and Iraq. He knew the difference between the sound of an incoming round that was close and the sound of one that was *really* close. That was the sound he was hearing now. Repeatedly.

Strueker *had* to get the convoy back to base. Not only did the ranger compound mean security, it meant medical attention for the wounded private whom his convoy had to evacuate.

The mission had started out like most others they had done in this dusty third world country up to that point. Special ops forces would be inserted by helicopter at the objective, usually a building somewhere in the city that Intel believed to contain Somali warlord Mohammed Farah Aidid or his henchmen. Rangers would surround the building while special operations forces went inside to look for militiamen. Then a convoy of Humvees and other army vehicles would show up to truck out the detainees. It was what they called their "mission template," and it had worked very well on the actions they had run up to this point.

Then Blackburn missed the rope.

On this mission, the rangers were to deploy around the target building by fast-rope from Black Hawk helicopters piloted by the U.S. Army's elite Night Stalkers. Fast-roping consists of wearing heavy leather gloves and sliding down a thick green rope from a hovering aircraft to the ground. It is an extremely quick and effective way to insert troops.

On this mission, however, tragedy struck. Private Blackburn had missed the rope, fallen seventy feet, and ended up sprawled in the dusty street with a broken back. Part of the vehicle convoy had to be split from the main group to evacuate him back to base. Sergeant Strueker had been put in command of this detachment. With three Humvees, each armed with a turret-mounted machine gun or grenade launcher, they had retrieved Blackburn and started back to the airfield where the rangers were housed. It should have been a short drive, but they had started encountering makeshift roadblocks and very heavy enemy fire.

When the three vehicles turned onto Halwadig Road, they were less than two miles from the base, but what they saw made Strueker's heart sink.

A mob of over ten thousand people blocked their way. It didn't seem like there was any possible way to get through.

So he started to improvise.

He threw a few flash-bang grenades out in front of the Humvee. That got the locals in the near vicinity to move, but he didn't have enough grenades to make it through the entire mob. So he had his gunner open up with the fifty-caliber machine gun over the heads of the crowd. It looked like God parting the Red Sea. The convoy sped up again. Then a truck full of local men blocked their path. When the pickup wouldn't move aside, he told his driver to ram it. It didn't take long for the Humvee to push the truck out of the way, and minutes later they were entering the safety of the base.

Medical personnel swarmed around them. Strueker got out and directed them to the middle Humvee, where Blackburn was. Then he grabbed an orderly. "I've got a dead man in the back of my vehicle. Someone needs to get him out of there."

The dead soldier was Dominick Pilla. He had been riding with Strueker for two months, and, as the medics removed the body from his badly shot-up Humvee, Strueker realized that he had never told Pilla about his faith.

Jeff Strueker had given his life to Christ at age thirteen. He grew up in a non-Christian household and his single mother had moved their family more than fifteen times before he graduated, so he had never stayed in one school or state for very long. One of those moves took him to Gallatin, Tennessee. Some neighbors took him to church several times and shared the gospel with him, and he accepted Christ. A month later his mother moved their family to Texas, and he never had much involvement with the church after that until he got into the army. There he found an active community of believers in Columbus, Georgia, right next to Fort Benning.

During the two months that the 3rd Ranger Battalion had been deployed to Somalia, Strueker had faithfully studied his Bible, and it was no secret among his fellow soldiers that he was a follower of Christ.

But as he stood looking at Pilla's lifeless body, he realized that simply practicing his faith had not been enough.

He started to pray, thanking God for delivering them to safety through the horrific gauntlet they had just run.

Just then, his platoon leader came over to him with some news that made him feel like eels were swimming in his stomach.

"Sergeant Strueker," he said. "A Black Hawk has been shot down in the city. You are going to have to get your men and go back out there to help with the rescue."

He had thought the mission was over. Now he realized that it was just beginning.

Strueker sent his men to get more ammunition and fuel. Then he and two others went and began to clean their friend's blood out of the back of his Humvee with water and brushes, knowing that if they didn't, it would have a serious psychological effect on the men who would be riding when they went back out.

As he attended to the job at hand, he began again to pray. His prayer was a pretty simple one, something like *God, what do I do now?* He didn't see any way that they could go back out into that hostile city and survive. It became crystal clear to him that this was the day that he would die. This would be his blood tomorrow. He thought about his wife of two years, Dawn. He had just received a letter from her, informing him that she was pregnant with their first child. He realized that he was never going to see the baby that he and Dawn had longed for.

Then he remembered something that he had read in his Bible that very week. It was the story of the Crucifixion, and Christ in the Garden of Gethsemane. He remembered the prayer that Christ had prayed in His darkest hour. "My Father, if it is possible, may this cup be taken from me." And that became Jeff Strueker's prayer.

But then he remembered the rest of Christ's prayer in the garden, and it pierced his soul. "Yet not as I will, but as You will." So he prayed, "God, I don't know what is going to happen next, but let Your will be done."

Strueker had never doubted that he was going to heaven, but at that moment everything that he said he believed came into perspective. He realized that whether he lived or died that day, he was in God's hands either way. He also knew without a doubt that if he died, God would take care of his wife and baby.

At that moment, Jeff Strueker knew peace. He was no longer afraid. As his men piled back into the Humvee, bristling with fresh ammunition, his prayer changed to a petition. "Please, God, don't let another one of my men die before someone shares the gospel with him." He was still convinced that he'd never see the morning, but he prayed with terrific urgency that God would spare the rest of his men.

During the next fourteen hours, Strueker's convoy came under heavy attack many times. At one point a rocket-propelled grenade skipped across the hood of the Humvee without exploding. Two Somalis opened up on them with machine guns from about ten feet away and completely missed.

When it was all over, three of the Humvee's tires were flat, and there was hardly a square foot of it that hadn't been pierced by a bullet, but, except for several minor wounds, not one of his men was seriously injured.

Eighteen men of Task Force Ranger did give their lives in that battle, however. It was the worst firefight that the U.S. had seen since the Vietnam War. When it was all over, Strueker had an amazing experience.

Men in his unit who had wanted nothing to do with God before were coming to him for answers. Rock-hard rangers who had no faith of their own were walking up with tears in their eyes, needing to draw on his faith to make sense of the tragedy. They wanted to know what happened to their friends who died and what would happen to them if tomorrow it was their turn? Many asked how God could allow this to happen.

Strueker and a Christian buddy spent the better part of the next forty-eight hours sitting on their bunks in the hangar while men lined up to talk to them about God.

It was then that God changed the direction of this sergeant's life. Strueker realized that in coming so near to death he had found a new reason to live. He had to share with other soldiers how they could have the peace that he had known under fire. He was seeing firsthand how badly men *need* a foundation of faith to allow them to persevere when the bullets are flying.

Today, more than nine years after that fateful deployment, Jeff Strueker has traded in his infantryman's insignia for a chaplain's cross. He currently serves with the 82nd Airborne. Just by looking at his badge-adorned uniform, the soldiers whom he counsels know that he has done the things that they are doing. In 1986 he won the Army's Best Ranger competition. He is a real-life action figure. But, lest the young soldiers in his care begin to believe that Jeff is the hero of his story, Strueker points to the cross on his lapel and tells them, "None of the badges on my uniform means anything compared to this."

As he prepares his unit spiritually for war, he tells them, "I don't care how tough you think you are, there is a situation out there in combat that will bring you to your knees. And when that time comes, you're going to need what I have."

Jeff Strueker is on a mission.

DELTA ALERT

★ ★ ★

ELLIE KAY

On September 11, while the president talked of war, our air force base went to Delta Alert, the most severe alert possible. All leaves were canceled as we, along with the rest of the nation, held our breath and waited for what came next. I was a fighter pilot's wife, and we'd long had our affairs in order. Yet I didn't expect my husband's reaction. Bob came home after flying later that week, closed the doors to my home office, and sat on the couch.

He tensely and abruptly asked, "Beloved, what if I don't come back?"

I was surprised at the question because he'd always taken his dangerous career in stride. But there is something different about this war on terrorism. Suddenly, I felt courage well up within me as I confidently answered him, "I believe you *will* come back, beloved. I believe that if you go, you'll have a job to do over there—you'll fly and fight and accomplish your mission. But I believe God still has a job for you back here, too."

My conviction and faith acted as a balm for Bob. He sighed, relaxed his shoulders, and said, "All right." He had confidence in his wife's prayers and that's all that he needed.

As soon as I spoke the last words to Bob, I sensed another profound thought deep within me. It was a still, small voice, filled with comfort and grace. *And even if he doesn't come back, it will still be all right.* But I didn't speak those words to Bob. Not then. Not there.

I know that there are no guarantees in life—whether you're a fighter pilot or a freelance writer. But I also know that faith in God is something that will carry us through anything this life throws at us. It isn't always easy, but it can be all right.

~

God is our refuge and our strength,
an ever-present help in trouble.

FROM THE BIBLE
PSALM 46:1

BROTHERS

★ ★ ★

GARY WALSH

> *"We few, we happy few, we band of brothers.*
> *For he today that sheds his blood with me shall be my brother."*
> SHAKESPEARE, *KING HENRY V*

The days of summer in the Sinai Peninsula can bake the energy and the hope clean out of a body. Our battalion, 1-505th Airborne, had weathered the first three months of the new Multinational Force and Observers mission in 1982, watching over the transition of the peninsula from Israeli to Egyptian control. The excitement of a prospective conflict had passed, and we settled in for the tedium of watching the desert simmer.

My family life was even more barren than the wasteland of the Sinai. I fully intended on divorcing my wife, Rita, after returning to Fort Bragg from the six-month deployment. Pride and selfishness were in full control of my life. I was lost in the wilderness, much as the Israelites had been for forty years. Then God sent a pillar of smoke in the shape of a former East Tennessee State linebacker.

Gary was a company commander, a great leader, and an even better teacher. We had an instant bond because we shared the same first name. I spent a lot of time with him at the various observation posts throughout the desert and back at the base camp. We worked out, went scuba diving, and most importantly, talked about life. Gary followed Christ in a compelling but winsome manner. We were the same age, the same rank, but his maturity put him years ahead of me. I found myself following his lead in many ways, especially when he pointed me back in the direction of my Savior.

I would like to say that I accepted Christ during that wilderness experience and was baptized in the Jordan. Unfortunately, I was stubborn and a slow learner. I didn't start following Christ until 1985 and didn't get serious about the relationship until October 1993 in Mogadishu, Somalia. But Gary was the pathfinder that pointed me in the right direction.

On a balmy evening in Mogadishu, two days after the battle that became popularly known as Black Hawk Down, I dropped off a letter to Rita in the Joint Operations Center of Task Force Ranger. Our marriage was growing stronger, through God's grace, but still had room for improvement.

I headed to the hangar that served as home for more than four hundred special operators and saw a small group of commanders standing in a circle, talking. A bright flash and a deafening blast drove me to the ground, paralyzed with the sheer surprise of the attack. Then I heard the screams of the wounded.

The lights had been turned off, so I used a mini-Mag Lite hanging from my neck on a suspension cord. The first wounded man that I saw was my brother in Christ, Gary. He was a squadron commander who had survived the intense combat of the Battle of Bakara Market, only to be cut down by a 60-mm mortar round. I clenched the Mag Lite between my teeth and began cutting away Gary's desert cammie trousers. The unsteady light revealed massive wounds to the thigh of one leg and the calf of the other. Shortly, six men were working with grim determination to keep Gary from bleeding out on us. The same round had wounded five other leaders and each was being cared for by some of the most professional soldiers in the world.

When we placed Gary on a helicopter for evacuation to the hospital at the UN compound, I truly believed that I would never see him alive again. It was a long night at our base at the airport, punctuated by an attempt by Somali militia to penetrate our perimeter. The shock of the attack on top of the trauma of the battle two days earlier bore down on Task Force Ranger like a heavy fog, permeating every fiber of our being. That is when prayer became very real to me.

Up to that day of my life, I had been on my knees only when it came to that point in the Mass when everybody else knelt down. I spent a lot of time that evening on my knees, praying for healing of all the wounded, but especially for the man who figuratively picked me up from the dusty desert in the Sinai. My uniform and boots were soaked with his blood. My life had been changed by his compassion.

Gary survived, but just barely. We put him on a C-141, bound for the military hospital at Landsthul, Germany, then on to Walter Reed Army Medical Center. His road to recovery was long and bumpy. Through God's grace and the love of his wife, children, and friends, Gary went back to full throttle and is now leading special operations forces in decisive battles against the evil forces of terrorism and fascism.

Of the other men wounded, one died. These brothers have been bonded not only by the combat that Shakespeare spoke of, but also by a common sense of duty and calling to follow Jesus Christ. If you are in the military, look around. You will find these brothers (and sisters), just like I found my brother Gary in the wilderness. Follow them, and follow Christ.

HONOR
AND
SACRIFICE

★★★

EPITAPH

When you go home,
Tell them of us, and say—
For your tomorrow,
We gave our today.

EPITAPH ON 2ND DIVISION MEMORIAL,
KOHIMA, BURMA, 1944
ATTRIBUTED TO JOHN EDMONDS

I CAME TO SEE
MY SON'S NAME

JIM SCHUECKLER

My job as a volunteer visitor guide was to help people find names on the "Moving Wall," a replica of the Vietnam Veterans Memorial in Washington, D.C. More importantly, I gave visitors a chance to talk. While searching the directory or leading a visitor to the name they sought, I would quietly ask, "Was he a friend or relative?" Over the six days, I began conversations that way with several hundred people. Only a handful gave me a short answer; almost everyone wanted to talk.

Each had their own story to tell. For some, the words poured out as if the floodgates of a dam that had been closed for thirty years had just burst open. For others, the words came out slowly and deliberately between long pauses. Sometimes, they choked on the words and they cried. I also cried as I listened, asked more questions, and silently prayed that my words would help to heal, not to hurt.

"I came to see my son's name." I heard those and similar words from several parents who came to the Moving Wall. Their son had died in a war that divided our country like no other event since the Civil War. He died in a war that some Americans had blamed on the soldiers who were called to fight it. Some young men had no choice; they were called by the draft. Others, including some thirty-thousand women, were called differently, by a sense of duty to their family and nation. Our culture mourns and respects our dead; but in the shadow of that bitter war, the sacrifices, of those who died and of their families, were not given dignity. Mothers and fathers came to see that their sons had not been forgotten, that their names were remembered on that wall, that someone else cares.

A frail and elderly mother came to the Moving Wall in a wheelchair. As we looked for her son's name, she described his interests during high school and then the agonizing days when she was first told that her son was injured, then missing, then classified as "lost at sea." She asked me to thank all the other people who helped bring the Moving Wall to Batavia.

"Till death do us part" came abruptly to thousands of marriages because of that war. I met two widows of men whose names are on the wall. One woman showed me a picture of her husband and a separate picture of their daughter—a daughter that her husband never met—a girl who grew up without a father. I was painfully aware that, had some Viet Cong soldiers been slightly better marksmen, my wife and son might have come to the wall to see my name.

Sisters and brothers came to see a name. One brother so close in age that he claimed "People were always calling us by the other's name, and we both hated it." A sister said, "I was so much younger than him, I didn't realize why my mom was crying when we said good-bye to him at the airport."

A group of four people stood near one panel. I offered to make a rubbing of a name. The man pointed to the name Paul D. Urquhart.

I asked, "Is that Captain Paul Urquhart, the helicopter pilot?"

The man nodded and said, "He's my brother."

I explained that I flew with Paul on his first tour in Vietnam and read that he had been shot down during his second tour. Paul's brother said that he and his family came from Pennsylvania on the anniversary date of Paul's becoming Missing In Action. I made a rubbing of Paul's name and added a rubbing of the Army Aviator wings from my hat, a symbol we had both worn so proudly so long ago.

Aunts and uncles also came to see a special name on the wall. One aunt said, "He stayed overnight at our house so much that one neighbor thought he was our son."

Cousins came to the wall; and many said, "He was like a brother."

One man asked me to look up the name Douglas Smith.

I asked back, "Do you mean Doug Smith, a marine, from North Tonawanda High School?"

The man introduced me to his wife, Doug's cousin. She was pleased to be able to talk about Doug with a classmate who remembered him. I showed her Doug's name on my own personal list.

Veterans came to see the names of their buddies. Most of them were eager to tell me about their friend or how he died. Many remembered the day in great detail and spoke of what's called "survivor's guilt."

"He went out on patrol in my place that day" or "If I hadn't been away on R & R [rest and recuperation], he wouldn't be dead."

Others were bothered that they couldn't remember much about their friend because they had tried to block it out for so many years. Another man said, "I lost a few good friends while I was there, but I don't want to find their names because I feel the same about all 58,000 of these names."

Many people came to the wall in the privacy or serenity of darkness. Our security men reported that there were only a few minutes each night that the wall had no callers at all. One visitor spent several hours in the middle of the night standing in front of a certain panel. Whenever anyone came close, he would move away. When alone again, he would move back to that panel to continue his silent vigil. Still others came in the darkness before dawn to watch the break of a new day over the wall.

Many people came who were not related to but knew one or more of the men named on the wall. A high school teacher told me, "I taught four of these boys."

Others said,

"He was the little boy who lived across the street."
"We were going steady in high school."
"He delivered my newspapers."
"I was his Boy Scout leader."
"He went to our church."
"I worked with his mother at the time he was killed."
"My son played football with him."
"We were classmates for twelve years."

There were hundreds of similar, personal connections between the visitor and one or more names on the wall.

Two weeks after the visit of the Moving Wall to Batavia, a friend told my wife, "I don't understand all the concern about the Moving Wall; why don't people just forget about that dirty war?"

For many, the Moving Wall does not need to be explained. Those who do not understand are, perhaps, more fortunate than those who do.

~

*The willingness with which our
young people are likely to serve in any war,
no matter how justified, will be directly
proportional to how they perceive the veterans
of earlier wars were treated and
appreciated by their nation.*

GEORGE WASHINGTON

THE BOYS OF IWO JIMA

★ ★ ★

MICHAEL T. POWERS

Each year my video production company is hired to go to Washington, D.C., with the eighth-grade class from Clinton, Wisconsin, where I grew up, to videotape their trip. I always enjoy visiting our nation's capitol and each year I take some special memories back with me. But this fall's trip was especially memorable.

On the last night of our trip, we stopped at the Iwo Jima memorial. It is the largest bronze statue in the world and depicts one of the most famous photographs in history—the World War II image of the six brave men raising the American flag at the top of Mount Surabachi on the island of Iwo Jima, Japan. About one hundred students and chaperones piled off the buses and headed toward the memorial. I noticed a solitary figure at the base of the statue, and as I got closer he asked, "Where are you guys from?"

"Wisconsin," I replied.

"Hey, I'm a Cheesehead too! Come gather around, Cheeseheads, and I will tell you a story."

James Bradley just happened to be in Washington, D.C., to speak at the memorial the following day. He was there that night to say good night to his dad, who has since passed away. He was just about to leave when he saw the buses pull up. I videotaped him as he spoke to us and received his permission to share what he said from my videotape. It is one thing to tour the incredible monuments filled with history in Washington, D.C., but it is quite another to get the kind of insight we received that night. When all had gathered around, he began to speak reverently.

"My name is James Bradley and I'm from Antigo, Wisconsin. My dad is on that statue, and I just wrote a book called *Flags of Our Fathers*. It is the story of the six boys you see behind me. Six boys raised the flag."

That's when he pointed to the guy putting the pole in the ground and told us his name was Harlon Block. "Harlon was an all-state football player. He enlisted in the Marine Corps with all the senior members of his football team. They were off to play another type of game, a game called war. But it didn't turn out to be a game. Harlon, at the age of twenty-one, died with his intestines in his hands."

Bradley shared that detail with us because he said that generals stand in front of the statue and talk about the glory of war. "You guys need to know that most of the boys in Iwo Jima were seventeen, eighteen, and nineteen years old.

He pointed again to the statue. "You see this next guy? That's Rene Gagnon from New Hampshire. If you took Rene's helmet off at the moment this photo was taken, you would find a photograph in the webbing. A photograph of his girlfriend. Rene put that in there for protection because he was scared. He was eighteen years old. Boys won the battle of Iwo Jima. Boys. Not men."

The next image on the statue was that of Sergeant Mike Strank. "Mike is my hero. He was the hero of all these guys. They called him the 'old man' because he was so old. He was already twenty-four. When Mike would motivate his boys in training camp, he didn't say, 'Let's go kill the enemy' or 'Let's die for our country.' He knew he was talking to little boys. Instead he would say, 'You do what I say, and I'll get you home to your mothers.'"

The next man on the statue was Ira Hayes, a Pima Indian from Arizona who lived through the terror on Iwo Jima. "Ira Hayes walked off Iwo Jima. He went into the White House with my dad, and President Truman told him, 'You're a hero.' He told reporters, 'How can I feel like a hero when 250 of my buddies hit the island with me, and only 27 of us walked off alive?'

"So you take your class at school. 250 of you spending a year together having fun, doing everything together. Then all 250 of you hit the beach, but only 27 of your classmates walk off alive. That was Ira Hayes. He had images of horror in his mind.

"The next guy, going around the statue, is Franklin Sousley from Hilltop, Kentucky, a fun-lovin' hillbilly boy," Bradley continued. "Franklin died on Iwo Jima at the age of nineteen. When the telegram came to tell his mother that he was dead, it went to the Hilltop General Store. A barefoot boy ran that telegram up to his mother's farm. The neighbors could hear her scream all night and into the morning. The neighbors lived a quarter of a mile away."

Finally Bradley pointed to the statue's image of his father, John Bradley from Antigo, Wisconsin. His dad lived until 1994, but declined all interviews. "When Walter Cronkite or the *New York Times* would call, we were trained as little kids to say, 'No, I'm sorry, sir, my dad's not here. He is in Canada fishing. No, there is no phone there, sir. No, we don't know when he is coming back.' My dad never fished or even went to Canada. Usually he was sitting right there at the table eating his Campbell's soup, but we had to tell the press that he was out fishing. He didn't want to talk to the press. You see, my dad didn't see himself as a hero. Everyone thinks these guys are heroes 'cause they are in a photo and on a monument. My dad knew better. He was a medic. John Bradley from Wisconsin was a caregiver. In Iwo Jima he probably held over two hundred boys as they died, and when boys died in Iwo Jima, they writhed and screamed in pain."

Bradley recalled his third grade teacher calling the elder Bradley a hero. "When I went home and told my dad that, he looked at me and said, 'I want you always to remember that the heroes of Iwo Jima are the guys who did not come back. DID NOT come back.'

"So that's the story about six nice young boys," Bradley finished. "Three died on Iwo Jima, and three came back as national heroes. Overall, seven thousand boys died on Iwo Jima in the worst battle in the history of the Marine Corps. My voice is giving out, so I will end here. Thank you for your time."

That number boggled my mind as I tried to comprehend how many lives those deaths altered back on American soil so many years ago. How many hearts of loved ones left behind were seared? Loved ones like this proud son who had so graciously shared part of his history with us.

Suddenly the monument wasn't just a big old piece of metal with a flag sticking out of the top. It came to life before our eyes through the heartfelt words of a son who did indeed have a father who was a hero then...and now.

A nation reveals itself not only
by the men it produces
but also by the men it honors,
the men it remembers.

PRESIDENT JOHN F. KENNEDY

SHOULD THE
OCCASION ARISE

Lt. Col. Donald S. Lopez, USAF (Retired)
From *Into the Teeth of the Tiger*

A Letter Home by Lieutenant John Beaty

Flying shark-mouthed P-40 fighters in the skies over China in 1943 and 1944, the men of the 23rd Fighter Group of the 14th Air Force participated in one of the most remarkable air campaigns of World War II. Their successors would become legendary as the decorated "Flying Tigers."

On December 12, 1943, the fighter squadron was scrambled to intercept a flight of Japanese bombers and accompanying fighter planes, called Zeros. Lieutenant John Beaty was shot down and killed on this mission, his first with the unit. He had joined the squadron only a few days earlier. The night before the mission, however, he wrote this letter, to be mailed only if he was killed:

Dear Mom, Dad, Sis, and Bud:

Tomorrow morning I go on what I hope will be the first of many missions. I'm a bit excited anticipating a thrill and content with my lot.

If this first mission, and those to follow, are fortunate for me, you'll never get this. I'm confident it never will be mailed, but should the occasion arise, I want you to have a message from me a little more personal than the adjutant general's—"REGRET TO INFORM YOU."

Naturally, I can't give you the details, nor do I consider them important, but I want to reassure you as to my "feelings" about the matter.

Should you get this, consider me just as alive as when I left the kitchen to milk the cow, or as when I carried the watermelon out to the stone table in the backyard, or as when I left you at the Grand Central that last time. After all, I have been away for a long time and this will just announce that I have gone to a better tour of duty, which will last a little longer, but which will end with our being together again.

I'd hate to think of your grieving over this prolonged separation, so look on it as I do. I've always yearned for far-off places and so-called adventures, and this is exactly what I want to satisfy that yearning.

There's a war going on and I'm where every man should want to be. What more could I ask? I don't have any particular aim after the war except a vague "I'd like to stay in the army" or "Guess I'll go to South America." The main reason I want to come home is to see you all. So remember when you miss me, that, while I'd just as soon live out my normal span and see more of you all, I did to the end what I've tried to do and "fought the good fight."

More than likely they'll send you some of my personal effects—my camera, my diary, my photos of you all and, possibly, my personal pistol, and my watch (if they find it). And so I've left enough trinkets behind that each of you should have a souvenir.

Don't weep over these manifestations of my physical existence, if you want me, just sit down in Dad's chair, in front of the fireplace, about midnight, and as the little blue flames dance above the coals, I'll be there, 'cause that's my favorite place in the world, especially since I hit China and the cold weather.

I hope Bud doesn't get into this business. He will make a name for himself in a peaceful world and I'd rather he did not have his sensibilities dulled. But if he does get in I know he'll make us all proud of him.

It would be nice to have a closer view of Sis, as she makes her place in the world. When I last saw her, she was becoming a woman and the sight was good to see.

Mom and Dad, I think the two of you are the best I've ever seen. You have given me the things I don't think I could have found anywhere else. I love and respect you more than anything else in the world and no mere separation of my soul from my body can dim that love.

There are many people I love and whom I'd like to enjoy life with. It would take a page to name them, but you know who the most important ones are and you'll tell them good-bye for me.

I hope it will be many years before we meet again. Where I am, that is but a moment and those years will be sweet for you. I love you all more than I can ever put into words, so until we meet again, God be with you.

Jack

COURAGE

$$\bigstar \ \bigstar \ \bigstar$$

AUTHOR UNKNOWN

I t was a few weeks before Christmas 1917. The beautiful snowy land-scapes of Europe were blackened by war.

The trenches on one side held the Germans and on the other side the trenches were filled with Americans. It was World War I. The exchange of gunshots was intense. Separating them was a very narrow strip of no-man's-land. A young German soldier attempting to cross that no-man's-land had been shot and had become entangled in the barbed wire. He cried out in anguish, then in pain he continued to whimper.

Between the shells all the Americans in that sector could hear him scream. When one American soldier could stand it no longer, he crawled out of the American trenches and on his stomach crawled to that German soldier. When the Americans realized what he was doing they stopped firing, but the Germans continued. Then a German officer realized what the young American was doing and he ordered his men to cease firing. Now there was a weird silence across the no-man's-land. On his stomach, the American made his way to that German soldier and disentangled him. He stood up with the German in his arms, walked straight to the German trenches, and placed him in the waiting arms of his comrades. Having done so, he turned and started back to the American trenches.

Suddenly there was a hand on his shoulder that spun him around. There stood a German officer who had won the Iron Cross, the highest German honor for bravery. He jerked it from his own uniform and placed it on the American, who walked back to the American trenches. When he was safely in the trenches, they resumed the insanity of war.

~

*The soldier above all other people
prays for peace, for he must suffer
and bear the deepest wounds and scars of war.*

GENERAL DOUGLAS MACARTHUR

ALWAYS FAITHFUL

★★★

CAROLE MOORE

Sergeant Rick Blankenship was a U.S. Marine and the only man Debby had ever loved. The two married as soon as she graduated from high school in the army town of Fayetteville, North Carolina, and settled into the transient military lifestyle. Eventually, Rick was stationed at Camp Lejeune Marine Corps Base in Jacksonville, North Carolina, not far from their hometown.

The year was 1983 and the Middle East boiled over with conflict. Soon Rick's unit received orders to take part in a peacekeeping mission in Beirut, Lebanon.

Rick packed his bags, kissed his young wife and two-year-old son, and settled into the marine barracks in Beirut. Personal computers weren't part of the landscape yet, so Rick and Debby kept in touch with frequent letters. Then, on September 17, 1983, on the occasion of their fifth wedding anniversary, Rick called home. They talked for an hour. It was the last time the two would speak.

On October 23, 1983, Debby and her mother were on an annual out-of-town shopping trip when they heard the news that the barracks was targeted by a suicide bombing. Certain Rick was away from the barracks on a training exercise, Debby didn't worry. But her confidence was premature—

before the day was out she was notified that Rick, along with 240 others, had died in the terrible bomb blast.

Debby was devastated. Pulling up stakes, she moved and kept on moving, always searching for something to take away the pain of losing her only love. Finally, she settled in Nashville.

Debby wasn't looking for love the night she met Eric Horner. A friend insisted she accompany him to a small club where Eric, the band director for country singer Lee Greenwood, played with a small group. But she couldn't help finding the tall, good-looking man with the mesmerizing voice and lightning-fast guitar compelling.

The two dated and finally wed. Then, on September 11, 2001, the World Trade Center collapsed as Debby sat and watched, transfixed. All she could think of was how much the incident reminded her of the bombing that cost her marine husband's life.

Debby pulled up photos of the Beirut bombing on the Internet and showed them to Eric, who realized for the first time just how deeply his wife still felt her loss. Inspired by Debby, he retired to his home studio, where he penned and recorded a patriotic song entitled, "We Will Stand."

On October 23, 2001, Eric, an accomplished country and gospel performer, sang at the annual memorial service honoring the men who died in Beirut. But he wanted to do more. When the Horners returned home to Nashville, he started working on another song, dedicated to Rick and the rest of the men who died in Beirut. Called "Always Faithful," it takes its name from the Marine Corps motto, Semper Fidelis. One line reads:

"It takes a heart of courage, a hero through and through, a patriot, a soldier, the proud and the few, Semper Fi."

Eric gave free use of the song for fundraising purposes to the foundation that supports the Beirut Memorial built in Jacksonville entirely from community donations. The following year, Debby watched as Eric stood beneath the towering statue of a marine in combat gear, elevated on a platform before a wall carved with the names of the men who died at the hands of terrorists in Beirut and sang a song dedicated to the first man his wife ever loved.

Did Eric feel strange paying tribute to Rick? Not at all, says Eric. "This is a guy who laid down his life for his country. He's a hero."

At Graveside

★★★

Scripture, prayers,
uniformed pallbearers,
taps by a lone bugler
Country's flag crisply folded
to a tight triangle; tenderly
presented, "On behalf of a
grateful nation…"
Hearts at half-mast—
indescribable grief
Loved ones and friends
held close to
the heart of God

CHARLOTTE ADELSPERGER

MY REMEMBRANCE
OF LIBERATION

JOHN SLATTON
AS TOLD TO TRICIA GOYER

On May 5, 1945, when the war in Europe was winding down, I served as the gunner and radio operator for First Platoon of Troop D, 41st Cavalry Reconnaissance Squadron, Mechanized. I was the gunner and radio operator in Sergeant Harry Sander's armored car.

We left Katsdorf, Austria, early that morning. Our mission was to scout a route across the Danube River for our 11th Armored Division tanks. We hadn't been on the road for more than fifteen minutes when we came to a roadblock of fallen trees. Within minutes, we secured our position and cleared the trees, but just as we prepared to move forward, a little white car approached flying a white flag of surrender. A representative of the Swiss Red Cross drove, bringing the commandant of the Mauthausen concentration camp to meet our troops. The Red Cross worker assured us that the commandant wished to surrender the death camps in that area to General Patton.

Sergeant Albert Kosiek commanded our platoon at this time. Kosiek stated, "I directly represent General Patton, and *our* platoon will take command of the camps."

The commandant warned Kosiek that twenty-three men would not be enough to handle the many German soldiers. Kosiek's answer was firm: "Then you don't know my men." But at that time, Kosiek had no idea the horror we'd soon face.

Our armored trucks and jeeps approached the camps with caution, winding our way through the small community of St. Georgen. In the middle of the quaint town we discovered Camp Gusen. The camp consisted of wooden barracks, barbed wire fences, and entanglements. The German guards stood at attention as we neared, their gun muzzles facing downward. But before we had a chance to provide much help to the thousands of prisoners, we were forced to move on to the mother camp Mauthausen where more German guards were awaiting surrender.

My goodness. We didn't expect anything like what we witnessed at Mauthausen. It was horrible. Thick granite walls and prisons, designed to last a thousand years, covered the hillside. Skeletal prisoners were everywhere—both dead and alive. Those barely hanging on to life apparently knew we were coming, and as we approached a mob surrounded our vehicles.

Sergeant Kosiek spoke to the crowd in his native tongue of Polish. Cheers of those who understood rose after each sentence. A Jewish soldier, Rosenthal, spoke several dialects of Hebrew and German. Another soldier spoke Spanish to the many prisoners from Spain.

In the end, the people finally understood their freedom. And although we couldn't offer much help with our limited supplies and expertise, we promised medics and nurses, cooks and clergy, would arrive the next day.

When we returned to base camp that night, our platoon of twenty-three men had rounded up over two thousand German guards. Also journeying with us was a former prisoner. Lieutenant Jack Taylor, part of navy intelligence, had been captured and taken to Mauthausen many months prior. That night as he rode in my armored car, Lieutenant Taylor told me about evidence he'd buried in the campgrounds—other American GI dog tags he'd risked his life to save. Lieutenant Taylor also told me how he'd been in line for execution three times, and how each of those times a Russian soldier had pushed him out of the way, taking his place. The

Russians wanted to save him so that Taylor could reveal the Nazi atrocities to the world.

I will never forget that day of liberation. I have been back to the area twice. The first time was in 1975. The International Mauthausen Committee had invited three other liberators and me. The second time was in 1989 when a Swiss television documentary, "The Forgotten Savior," was filmed in honor of the Swiss Red Cross gentleman who'd led us to the camps.

Yet going back to Mauthausen was not easy. When I went back in 1975, one thing plagued me. The camp had monuments, statues, and memorials for all kinds of people—the Italians, French, Belgiums, British. But nothing was mentioned of the Americans, the ones who liberated the camp. I returned home with the determination that we were going to have some sort of a marker. Something to let future generations know about the deeds of the men I served with.

I went before Congress, but soon discovered Congress cannot spend money on overseas monuments. My next plan was to approach members of the 11th Armored Division Association for funds. Instead, when the International Mauthausen Committee and the Austrian government heard of our desire, the Austrian government agreed to pay for the plaque.

It's not a big thing, but we have a three-foot-by-five-foot marble marker attached to the prison walls, stating:

"In remembrance of the members of the 11th Armored Division of the Third U.S. Army who liberated the concentration camp at Mauthausen, Gusen, Ebensee, and others located nearby in Upper Austria in May 1945. Their deeds will never be forgotten."

It thrills me to know that plaque will always remain as a reminder—even after the last liberator has passed on. After all, it was an ordinary humanitarian worker who approached our armored column that sunny, May day. It was twenty-three ordinary soldiers who open the gates to freedom, bringing hope to thousands. And years later it was also just one ordinary veteran who made sure the deeds of his friends would never be forgotten.

OPEN DOOR TO FORGIVENESS

LIEUTENANT COLONEL MARK SIMPSON
UNITED STATES AIR FORCE

On September 2, 1958, an Allied intelligence listening post recorded the following transmission between Soviet air defense ground controllers and a flight of four MIG-17 interceptor pilots as they shot down an Air Force C-130 reconnaissance aircraft over Soviet Armenia:

582 "I see the target, a large one. Its altitude is 100 [10,000 meters] as you said."

201 "I am attacking the target."

201 "218... Attack! Attack! The target is a transport; four engine."

582 "The target is burning."

201 "218... Are you attacking?"

218 "Yes...I...[unintelligible]... The tail assembly is falling off the target..."

201 "Look at him; I will finish him off, boys; I will finish him off on the run... The target has lost control; it's going down."

End of transmission

Though I was only three months old at the time, this transmission was to have the most profound effect upon my life.

Ask people what they remember of the Cold War, and you will get a wide variety of answers. For many, Cold War memories revolve around the air raid drills of the late 1950s and early 1960s, around Gary Francis Powers, or around the Cuban Missile Crisis.

A younger generation may remember the Cold War only by the crumbling of the Berlin Wall. Unknown to many Americans, the Cold War was fought globally on many fronts. Many American military personnel made the ultimate sacrifice for global peace. U.S. crews manned nuclear components of the strategic triad while others stood at the ready with tactical weapon systems deployed around the world.

During the Cold War, a relatively small group of aviators made up of flight crews and airborne reconnaissance operators gathered information for the National Security Agency's Central Security Service. Eighteen types of air force and navy aircraft were shot down during the Cold War. Information on these missions, shrouded for decades in secrecy, was recently declassified.

As a young child in the sixties, the Cold War meant hiding under my desk at school. Later, as an air force navigator, I fought the Cold War aboard B-52 and B-1 bombers, while the nation was sitting at nuclear alert.

But most importantly for me, the Cold War had a darker meaning.

My father, Captain John E. Simpson, was a pilot who flew highly sensitive reconnaissance missions along the borders of the Soviet Union in the late 1950s. A few C-130As, widely known for their tactical aircraft role, were refitted to perform airborne signal reconnaissance. On September 2, 1958, one of these 130s flying the border of Turkey and the Soviet Union was shot down after being attacked by a flight of four MIG-17s. The entire crew of seventeen—six flight deck personnel and eleven reconnaissance operators—was lost. One of them was my father.

My mother was left in her mid-twenties with two boys—John Jr. (four years old) and me (three months). She knew nothing more than that her husband had died in a crash on a rocky hillside inside the Soviet Union. Later that fall, the family received word that negotiations between the two superpowers had resulted in six sets of remains being repatriated to the United States; four sets were positively identified. My father's remains were one of the four returned to their families in late 1958. The other two bodies were interred in Arlington National Cemetery in unknown graves.

Growing up, I developed a deep-seated hatred for the Russians—hatred fueled by world events and by family members. The hatred and bitterness that came from not knowing my father resulted in my adopting a rather rebellious lifestyle.

But God was at work, even though I didn't know it. I became a Christian during high school, though God still had a lot of work to do in my heart.

I left home for college and joined the Air Force ROTC. Upon joining, I was asked whether I had any reservations about delivering nuclear weapons. I responded coldly, "Not in the least. Where do I sign?" My initial military goals were to "nuke" the communists and to get the real story about my father.

I entered active duty in 1982 and began to hone my aeronautical skills. In the Strategic Air Command, I became one of the most accurate and deadly bombardiers in the force. My family had put my father on a pedestal. I made him into a god and was trying to worship him the best way I could.

Bitterness-induced darkness enveloped my life despite my Christian beliefs. I sought the world and my earthly father, and that blinded me spiritually for the first eight years of my air force career. As relations thawed between the U.S. and Soviet Union, I was surprised and confused.

The Cold War had been won, but my personal cold war was unresolved.

In 1993, the two superpowers began to exchange information on aircraft shot down during the previous fifty years. Russia finally admitted to shooting down the C-130 my dad was piloting. As documents were declassified, the cold war in my heart began to thaw.

The final chapter in the battle for my heart took place a year later. I was given the opportunity to share my story at a Bible study at the Air Combat Command Headquarters. That day three former Soviet officers sat in front of me. The Holy Spirit moved in my heart as I spoke. As I finished, I turned to those former enemies and asked them to forgive me for hating them and their people for so many years.

A broken spirit coupled with forgiveness opened the doors to healing, not only for me, but also, perhaps, for those ambassadors from Eastern Europe.

Several years later, I was reunited with the other war orphans who lost their fathers on that terrible day in 1958. We stood with families and friends as a memorial to their service was unveiled in Fort Meade, Maryland. The following day, my father was again remembered at Arlington National Cemetery. As the bugler sounded taps and guns sounded their final salute, we were able to close the door on their chapter of our lives.

As I drove away from the cemetery, tears, which had been choked back in the past, ran down my face. My eyes swept past the thousands of white headstones that stood in silent tribute to fallen compatriots. The Spirit reminded me that the living weren't there. My father was alive in heaven, and in that I took great comfort.

I rejoiced to feel alive again. The spirit of a heavy heart had been lifted and replaced with an unsurpassable peace. Jesus had fought and won my personal cold war. It was finished when I loosened my grip on the sword of bitterness and laid it at my Savior's feet.

SO MANY DREAMS

★ ★ ★

Diane Dean White

We met in high school during my senior year. He had ambitions for a career in the field of mechanics and engineering; he wanted to design cars someday. He enrolled in college but not before he received a letter from Uncle Sam inviting him to join in a war that was going on in Vietnam.

Basic training took place in Missouri and there was a brief leave before he reported for duty in Saigon. His parents were gone and he lived with his older sister and family. We shared times of laughter and fun with friends. Yet, too soon it was over and I drove him to the airport where he departed to join his battalion in California.

Over the next year while he was fighting a war, I was in college having fun with new friends. I always managed to get a letter to him, praying all was well. I received many letters that year; they were censored and he never mentioned his location. One was written in rice paddies and he described the area as if it were a lovely picturesque setting. Maybe during that moment it truly was for him, but I knew as an infantryman he was in the thick of it.

A year later, he was returning stateside so I offered to pick him up at the airport. Waiting for his arrival I noticed many young men coming home. Some were maimed and walking with a crutch to support one leg, others were wearing a sling holding their arm in place. Wives and girl-friends, parents and siblings waited patiently as planes arrived. Lovers were united, mothers cried and hugged their sons, and dads patted their shoulders, proud of their contribution in this war.

I guess he saw me first; the uniforms all looked the same. He was very handsome and mature as he walked up and gave me a hug. His face seemed to be older. His skin was tan, and when I looked into his eyes I knew he had lived a lifetime in that year.

On the way home he was hungry so we stopped at a little restaurant away from the busy airport and people. He ordered a hearty meal, and although I tried to get him to talk, he held back, often looking behind his shoulder. He stood out in his army uniform, others glanced often.

A man next to us asked him if he had seen action. He responded kindly and to the point, where he had been and for how long. I think the man would have continued, but his wife laid her hand on his arm.

We ate in silence, and although he only ate a portion of his food, he went to pay the bill. To his surprise the owner told him it had been taken care of by the man at the other table. My friend said, "Thank you, sir."

"No. Thank you, son." There was an exchange of understanding in their expressions.

After the ride back to his sister's, we kept in touch, but college was starting and I was leaving to go out of state. He had made plans to attend a school near home, using the GI bill to help with his tuition. It was some-time over a year later that I ran into him; he was happy and working at his studies. We talked, touching on the highlights of our lives, and finally said good-bye.

Another year went by and I was engaged to be married. I sent him an invitation, but he was attending a function with his girlfriend. I was happy to hear he had met someone.

Years went by and we lived states away from one another. The exchange of notes at Christmas was our only contact, until one year recently. It wasn't his signature. It was his wife's handwriting. There was also a newspaper clipping with it.

She wrote that although he seemed fine for many years after the war, in the midnineties he started having problems. He went to a hospital in Maryland to go through testing. Soon he started receiving treatments for Agent Orange. After several years they said there was nothing more they could do except make him comfortable. He had two grown children when he passed away at a young age. The clipping was his obituary.

My mind paused to remember the fun and banter we had and the little restaurant where the man bought our meal, and how proud and nice my friend looked in his uniform. There was never any question about his going to war; he was glad to do it for his country. It was just hard to believe that after over a year in battle, he once again had to battle another war. I mourned for the person who had so many dreams.

I responded with a letter of sympathy and shared some memories with his wife. It was a sad and cruel thing, but I knew he would have been brave about it, just like he was so many years ago when Uncle Sam had called him to serve in the sixties. This time he wasn't at battle any longer, the pain was gone, and it was the Lord who was finally calling him home.

A WARRIOR'S HEART

★ ★ ★

JEFF ADAMS

I always went to chapel and took communion, especially before a mission," Dad said. One day he listened to the message a little closer.

Flying over Europe in World War II, Dad did what soldiers do—his duty—but he longed to be with his family. Every day, half of the squadrons never returned. The planes were shot down; the crews were killed or captured. Everyone was afraid. No one wanted to die. But they had a job to do. So they did it.

On one particular mission, Dad was wounded. Their targets were in sight. The bomb bay doors were open. Flak burst all around them. The sky filled with thunderous puffs of black smoke and deadly shrapnel. Shards of burning metal pierced the windshields of the bombers, crippling and blinding pilots. Dad turned to look at an instrument panel to his right. A tiny jagged projectile grazed his left temple.

If he had not turned his head at that precise moment, he would have been hit squarely between the eyes, possibly killing him.

Afterward, he thought more about why he survived. Almost everyone went to church, even if they didn't believe in God. "We called it 'foxhole religion,'" Dad said. Whether soldiers were in foxholes or cockpits, when they knew they might die, they often became believers. For Dad, it wasn't too late.

At the next service, he gave thanks and received communion. The chaplain quoted from Matthew 10:28, "And fear not them which kill the body, but are not able to kill the soul: but rather fear him which is able to destroy both soul and body in hell."

Years later Dad told me, "You never knew who was going to be alive at the end of the day. I would have been killed instantly. I realized God was talking to me. I always asked God to spare my life, but I had never asked him to save my soul." He remained grateful the Lord answered his prayer that day.

Like so many men who have lived through a war, Dad didn't know why he survived and others—men he considered better than himself—died.

Two days after Dad departed Italy, his former plane was shot down. The pilot, the new copilot, and the entire crew were killed. Dad, an only son whose wife had become ill after the death of their infant son, returned home to the family his heart had never left.

INFERNO ON GREEN RAMP

MAJOR MARK LEE WALTERS, U.S. ARMY

arch 23, 1994, started off as an exceptionally great day. If you had asked me what my life's priorities were, I would have told you they were God, Stephanie, and the army. But if you had looked into my schedule book, even a casual observer would have seen otherwise. In fact, both Stephanie and God were competing for my leftovers—leftover time and leftover energy.

That particular morning I didn't spend time with the Lord because there was just too much to do. In two weeks I was going to take command of an airborne rifle company. I felt I needed every available moment to tie up loose ends at work and log as many parachute jumps as I could. I had allowed myself to let the tyranny of the urgent take the place of both God and family.

By that afternoon, I was one of about two hundred airborne soldiers at Pope Air Force Base conducting preflight preparations and rehearsals on the Green Ramp. On that taxi ramp we used aircraft mock-ups to practice the actions we performed in flight. It was a beautiful day; no wind, no clouds, the temperature near sixty degrees and the winds low; all in all, a perfect day for a jump.

Without warning our perfect day changed. Above us a C-130

Hercules transport aircraft received approval to land. At the same time, an F-16 mistakenly also received approval to land in the same direction. Neither pilot saw the other due to the angle they were coming from, and they collided. Miraculously, the C-130 was able to right itself. The F-16, however, went out of control and the pilots had to eject. The F-16 crashed and struck a parked aircraft. The ensuing fireball, debris, and exploding munitions engulfed the paratroopers training on the Green Ramp.

Our location prevented us from seeing the wall of fire coming our way. I only remember the expression of total disbelief in my jumpmaster's eyes when he yelled "An airplane is crashing toward us!" Instinctively, I dropped to the ground as the jet's fuselage roared past and a sheet of flame rolled over me. In the next instant the roar was replaced by the screams of those around me.

When I got up, I felt pain on the back of my hands and head. I knew my injuries weren't life threatening because I wasn't bleeding or on fire. The paratrooper next to me, however, had been thrown against a metal door and was bleeding profusely from his forehead. I used my jacket to stop the bleeding, kept talking to him, and tried to keep him from going into shock. At that point, I saw the destruction and carnage that surrounded me. I felt utterly helpless as I saw scores of paratroopers around me on fire or mortally injured from burns, blast, or airborne debris. Twenty-four were killed and more than one hundred injured. Later I learned that this was the worst training accident in the history of the division.

Eventually, I arrived at the hospital, where my wife, Stephanie, worked. I was placed in a makeshift treatment room, clearly a lower priority than the more seriously injured paratroopers. Many had burns covering up to 90 percent of their bodies or severe injuries from shrapnel.

I remember seeing Stephanie for the first time that day. When our eyes met, we could see mutual concern, coupled with relief. The unspoken encouragement I received from her eyes was overwhelming. She didn't have time to talk because she was busy carrying information from the hospital staff to the families of the victims.

I remained in the hospital at Fort Bragg for four days while they cleaned my wounds and evaluated me for further surgery and treatment. During this period, I experienced pain like I had never known. Twice daily I underwent wound debridement treatments. A therapist ran my hands under water and removed the burned tissue and dirt from my skin with a metal scraper. I forgot to take the pain medicine prior to the first treatment and thought I was going to pass out. I didn't forget to do that again.

Later, I was transferred with a number of the other paratroopers to Brooke Army Medical Center in Texas. There I received skin grafts to the backs of both my hands. Then I remained in traction for several days with arms braced and suspended from my shoulders to my fingertips to keep me from damaging the new skin.

Finally, I was allowed to go home and after thirty days on convalescent leave I was back in the harness. Later that summer, I took command of an airborne company.

Many asked me why I wasn't more upset or angry at the pilots or air traffic controllers for allowing this accident to occur. Certainly that is one response. What I took from that experience, however, was something quite different. For me I chose to relearn what was truly important and reset my priorities.

I don't really know why I was on the Green Ramp that day, or why God chose to spare me when men to my left and right were killed. The fact that God spared me means that His purpose in my life has not yet been fulfilled. I do know I will continue to live a life built on these words of the apostle Paul, "Forgetting what lies behind and reaching forward to what lies ahead, I press on toward the goal for the prize of the upward call of God in Christ Jesus" (Philippians 3:13–14).

THE BATTLE OF LEYTE

★★★

CURTIS LIDBECK
U.S. NAVY, GUNNER'S MATE THIRD CLASS

O ur Liberty ship, the S.S. *Alexander Majors,* was about to leave port, and I was in the base hospital in Dutch New Guinea. My tooth was infected, but after four days of high fever and a bad case of impatience, I cornered a nurse and told her I didn't care how she did it, but she would release me or I would be AWOL because they weren't going to leave without me.

When I boarded, the ship was loaded with troops and equipment for the invasion of Leyte. We were warned that there was submarine activity all through these waters. Since the Japanese would try to hold the Philippines at all costs, I knew that the next thirty days would change my life. I had been keeping a journal, and I decided to be sure to record what the coming days would bring.

NOVEMBER 3, 1944.
Today was quiet. We are close now. We all sleep near our guns and stay fully clothed including life jackets.

NOVEMBER 4, 1944.
We arrived in Leyte and around nine last night we were called to general quarters and had a continual air raid until the all-clear

signal at seven this morning. We saw many enemy aircraft shot down in flames. I tried with my 20-mm but do not know if I hit any. We all could use some sleep.

NOVEMBER 11, 1944.
We have been here a week now and had air raids every day and night but one. That particular night we had a raging typhoon. The ship had three anchors out, two forward and one stern, and we were still moving.

Today a fleet of our transport planes came in with three Zeros, or Japanese planes, hiding right behind them. There were three Liberty ships, including mine, in a row. The first one still had a hold full of soldiers. The Zero dove into the hold where the GIs were and blew up. The second dove into the ship ahead of us, and his five-hundred-pound bomb blew fire and metal high in the air. My friend slapped a magazine on his 20-mm and started shooting. His hit the third Zero. The plane banked and hit the sea.

NOVEMBER 12, 1944.
This was the day! Over four hundred suicide planes were headed for Leyte. We were tired when we saw wave after wave of these Zeros coming in. There were explosions and fire everywhere with many ships hit and certainly many lives lost. One dived and just missed our ship. Another dropped his bomb off our starboard side and rocked the ship.

I was in charge of all the guns on the ship except the five-inch 38 on the stern. All guns were firing all day, and finally as the planes were thinning out, there was one that was pretty high above our ship. Suddenly he went into a dive and was coming straight toward us. Everything in the harbor was firing at it, including me. How he kept coming through the barrage is unbelievable. Finally the five-inch 38 shot a projectile which was close enough to the plane to raise it just a bit, but not close enough to knock it down. It just missed the bridge and my gun but caught a wing on another part of the ship. His five-hundred-pound bomb blew up along with several barrels of high octane gasoline lashed nearby. There was fire and shrapnel everywhere.

I watched as some of the sailors were killed instantly; others jumped overboard. The gunnery officer told me to take any men who needed medical attention to shore facilities. By this time there were several boats headed our way to see if there was anything they could do. We loaded the injured men from the bow. We set off, and as I looked back at the burning ship with flaming gasoline pouring off, I could not see how the ship could survive. We met a white barge with a red cross on it and flagged it down. I transferred our men onto it to be taken to the hospital, and I caught another boat and asked to be taken back to the ship. I climbed aboard and everything was chaos.

An army repair ship had just come in from the States that day. It nosed our ship around so that the flames would be blown across the ship instead of toward the bridge, and that probably saved the *Alexander Majors*.

There was not enough left of the suicide plane to make a watchband. Burned into my memory will always be the sight of that spinning prop and streaking black smoke. I still shudder as I think of how imminent death can be.

Although the damage to our ship was extensive, we continued to fight in the heavy battle for the next two weeks. We had 162 air raids in the thirty days we were fighting in the Battle of Leyte. I never imagined before the relief it is to take a peaceful breath of air. I've heard of foxhole conversions, but I venture to say there were hundreds of gun-tub conversions in Leyte. I only hope these men do not forget their promises to God. I hope I never do. I was not a Christian during the war, but I learned how to pray. And I know God began a work in my life during that time that eventually led me to receive Christ as my own Savior. I felt God's presence and protection every minute of those thirty days in Leyte—thirty days I can never forget.

A WARRIOR'S PASSING

★★★

MAJOR ERIC KAIL, U.S. ARMY

I t was a warm sunny morning, like all the other mornings a young boy enjoys growing up in Hawaii. My dad had just returned from his second tour in Vietnam. He had served thirty-two years in the army, rising to the rank of colonel while commanding at the company battalion and brigade levels. The traditions, strengths, and values of the military were deeply embedded in him, and in turn, he taught them to me.

That day we were taking a trip that would forever define my impression of my dad's character. After a short drive, we stood as a family by a chain-link fence. We formed a small part of a large crowd that watched an airplane land on a military runway. I was only six, but I had seen planes land before, so I watched Dad's face for an explanation of what was special about this one.

After what seemed hours, the plane door opened and a couple of men in uniform walked down onto the runway. One of them even stopped for a moment to kiss the ground. He was one of the last returning POWs from Vietnam. Looking up to Dad, I stopped short of asking a question and instead simply stared at him.

The emotions I saw on his face defined in an instant the character I still strive to emulate: selfless pride in knowing that he was brother to these men; joy in the fact that their prayers had been answered; a brief sadness that they had been made to persevere through suffering for so long; and peace in the knowledge that their homecoming was at last taking place. That day remains my earliest and most lasting memory: It was also the beginning of a very young boy making a commitment to be like his father someday.

Dad was the epitome of an American country boy from the Midwest. He was honest, reliable, and brutally straightforward. Though never obsessed with perfection, he was a man committed to high standards and craftsmanship. When I was a young cadet, he gave me a verse that clearly explained his work ethic: "If racing against mere men makes you tired, how will you race against horses? If you stumble and fall on open ground, what will you do in the thickets near the Jordan?" (Jeremiah 12:5). On the day I graduated from Ranger school, he gave me a big hug and said, "Run with the horses, Bud!"

My dad identified strongly with a centurion named Cornelius mentioned in the Bible; a man of duty, leadership, and faith. Dad was a true warrior; therefore, he manifested an aggressive drive for the care and development of other warriors. He believed that sitting on the sidelines was a cheap way of life, so he consistently exhorted those he knew to get into the game. One of my favorite soldierly heirlooms from him hangs in my office doorway. No one can enter without seeing the small brass and wood plaque that reads, "Do *something*…lead, follow, or get out of the way!"

Dad had many passions. He loved his family and the great outdoors. He would stop whatever he was doing to brag about his grandkids or talk about fly-fishing and elk hunting. At the top of his list, however, was bringing the Good News of Christ to our military.

We said our last good-byes to my father as we buried him on a crisp November morning at Arlington National Cemetery. I will miss him. He left a legacy of faith and stewardship worthy of a prince. In our sorrow, we should follow his example of selfless pride that he was a brother in arms, joy that his prayer has been answered, brief sadness that he needed to persevere through suffering in the flesh, and peace knowing that his homecoming has taken place.

A SISTER'S PROMISE

★★★

HARRIETTE PETERSON KOOPMAN
AS TOLD TO CONNIE PETTERSEN

I was a month short of eighteen and my brother, Don, was sixteen on that day of infamy, December 7, 1941. Americans raced to join the armed services. My elder brothers, Bob and Orv, enlisted in the army, leaving Don and me the oldest of the seven siblings still at home.

We inherited the older boys' chores when they left for war, so we teamed up. Music and laughter made our work fun. Our teenage voices harmonized with the radio's popular war songs: "Don't Sit under the Apple Tree with Anyone Else but Me" and "I'll Be Seeing You."

By 1942, Orv and Bob were fighting overseas. After every letter home, Don started begging Pa to let him join the navy.

"I wanna go…my country needs me."

"You're not old enough!" Pa's face was ashen.

"You can sign when I'm seventeen."

"This war has two of my boys."

Don persisted many months, finally threatening to lie about his age. Reluctantly, Pa signed. Don joined the navy on his seventeenth birthday, November 3, 1942.

I couldn't bear another brother—especially Don—in such danger; so far away.

"Don," I begged him, "don't go."

"I have to, Sis. If the boys won't enlist, we'll never win. God's hand is in this war. It'll work out."

So sure, so grown up.

Don—short and wiry—became an aerial gunner with Navy Squadron VB 112 flying PB4Ys. I missed our chats and singing. I missed his laugh and gentle spirit. Every night, I'd ask God to send him a guardian angel.

Months passed. Seasons changed. Don's letters always closed with, "Sis...I'm in God's hands."

In June 1943, Don returned to St. Paul before deployment overseas. Several days into his leave, our folks went dancing. I played with the kids on the braided living room rug, but Don's thoughts seemed far away.

"Don, are you okay?" I asked. "Don't you like the navy?"

He smiled. "I like the navy, it's not that."

After the kids were asleep, we sat on the couch.

"If it's not the navy, what's wrong? Why aren't you with your friends?"

Don hesitated. "Sis, you gotta promise—don't tell Ma and Pa."

A secret. Just like old times.

"Sis, this is my last leave. I won't be coming home again. I'll be...giving my life for my country."

"How can you know that?" I asked, tears filling my eyes.

"It's...a feeling. A premonition. The Lord's given me peace about it."

After a prolonged silence—and swallowing the lump in my throat—I said, "If that's what you believe, then stay close to the Lord. Don't let go!"

"I will. That's why I wanna take in as much of home as I can."

We closed our eyes and prayed. Rested, together in His peace. His comfort.

Days later, our family gathered around Don at the train station, one by one, tearfully hugging him. When my turn came, I sang:

God be with you till we meet again;
When life's perils thick confound you;
Put His arms unfailing round you;
God be with you till we meet again.

Don joined the chorus, but choked up. Taking a deep breath—with tears streaming—he turned and ran for the train. He didn't look back.

On his eighteenth birthday, he shipped overseas. Based out of Port Lyautey, French Morocco, in North West Africa as an ordnance man and gunner with Crew #9, his crew practiced familiarization flights in their B-24 Liberator.

On his squadron's first combat mission, November 30, 1943, his plane attempted to return to base in dense fog from a successful Atlantic patrol mission guarding U.S. convoys to Italy. Don's crew repeatedly— unsuccessfully—tried to radio their base. Critically low on fuel, they crashed near Faro, Portugal.

The impact broke the plane apart, killing five crewmembers. Six survivors were pulled from the sea into a small boat guided by two Portuguese fishermen.

Don never made it out of the plane that night. He never came home again. And I never told Pa and Ma he knew he'd die for his country and be with God.

He was a brave American, a wonderful brother, and a faithful Christian who taught me to trust the Lord and look forward to heaven.

Because of the promise of the Resurrection and Don's courage, I don't fear death. I look forward to seeing Don and singing together once again:

Till we meet...at Jesus' feet...
God be with you till we meet again.

LOVE AND FAMILY

MOTHER'S COVERS

When you were small
And just a touch away,
I covered you with blankets
Against the cool night air.

But now that you are tall
And out of reach,
I fold my hands
And cover you in prayer.

BITSY BARNARD CRAFT

GOD'S PERFECT TIMING

★★★

BILL DIXON, U.S. ARMY MEDICAL CORP
SERVING IN OPERATION IRAQI FREEDOM
AS TOLD TO CHUCK HOLTON

Bill Dixon never expected to find himself living in an airport.

Especially this airport. It used to be called Saddam International, but a week before he arrived, U.S. forces captured it during the liberation of Iraq. It had promptly been renamed "Baghdad International," and was now being used as a staging area for missions into the city itself.

Bill is a doctor, a major in the U.S. Army Medical Corps, assigned to the 28th Combat Army Surgical Hospital. A month earlier he'd kissed his pregnant wife, Shannon, good-bye and told her not to worry, he hoped to be home before the baby was born. After all, their son wasn't due for more than two months.

While any separation from one's family is painful, Major Dixon counted his blessings. Unlike most of the troops in the field, Major Dixon had the great luxury of being able to call home once in a while—the unit had a satellite telephone, and everyone was given about five minutes a week to keep in touch with loved ones. He wasn't able to call for several weeks once the war started, however, as the C.A.S.H moved up behind the 101st Airborne Division, which was advancing on Baghdad. During that period, it was hard enough just to find time to sleep, much less talk on the telephone.

Once the unit arrived at Baghdad International and set up shop, Bill and the other medical personnel actually treated very few American soldiers. Instead, they saw a steady stream of patients from the surrounding area, mostly Iraqi women and children who were sick or injured. One patient in particular, though, hit home in Bill's heart.

A four-year-old girl, horribly burned from the explosion that killed her parents, came under his care. It was especially difficult for Bill, since his own daughter was four. Within days, as the little Iraqi girl struggled to live, her plight had captured the hearts of the entire unit.

As the weeks wore on, Bill got a strong feeling that he needed to call and check up on his wife. This day, especially, thoughts of Shannon kept coming to his mind.

He decided he had to call her. So he pleaded with the sat-phone operator to allow him a call and dialed his home number, grateful for the technology that allowed him to look in on his beloved from so far away. There was no answer.

Not overly concerned, he called Shannon's parents' house in Florida; she had planned to travel down there before the baby was born. Her father answered, and his voice had an urgent tone.

"You need to call the hospital, Bill. Shannon's medical condition has gotten worse, and they've decided that she needs to have the baby right now."

"What!" Bill almost shouted. "She's five weeks early!"

He quickly hung up and dialed the phone number that Shannon's father had provided for her room at the hospital.

In a delivery room at Bethesda Naval Hospital, a very sick Shannon Dixon was actively laboring, less than thirty minutes from delivering their baby. Her world brightened, though, when a doctor walked in and announced that they were transferring a phone call to her from Iraq. The unexpected news made her forget her misery for a moment, as she picked up the phone and heard Bill's voice say, "What are you doing, lady?"

They spoke for a few minutes, Bill apologizing for not being there to witness the birth, Shannon incredibly grateful that he had listened to the voice inside that told him to call.

Less than thirty minutes later, five-and-a-half pound John Henry Dixon took his first breaths, sporting big hands and feet like his daddy.

As for the little Iraqi girl, one of the nurses in the unit has asked to be allowed to adopt her if she lives, so that she can receive the medical treatment that she will need to be able to recover fully. It is certain that for every story of selfless generosity like this, there are many more that never get told.

And for Major Bill Dixon, while he'll always regret not being there for the birth of his son, he counts himself blessed to have been allowed to bring comfort to other children and is proud to serve a country where generosity, service, and love are given an honored place in its culture and history.

FADED PHOTOGRAPH

★ ★ ★

BOB HENDERSON
ST. PETERSBURG TIMES

Clair Miller and his crew picked up a new B-24 at California's March Field on Christmas Eve, 1943, and prepared to fly to England. But they decided to have "one more hamburger" before heading out for the distant land of fish and chips.

As the airmen sat in a local restaurant, a beautiful young waitress approached. "I understand you're going to England," she said to Miller. Then she told him that her fiancé, an aviation gunner like Miller, was stationed there.

The woman said she was waiting for him to provide an address so she could send him a picture of herself. "You might run into him," she told Miller hopefully. "Would you take it?"

Miller knew it was unlikely he'd ever see her fiancé. But he didn't want to disappoint the woman. He took the picture and placed it in his wallet. Later he realized he hadn't even asked the man's name. Then it was on to Europe and the war.

On August 9, 1944, Miller's plane was shot down, and he was forced to parachute to an island off the coast of Holland. Captured by the Nazis, he spent the next nine months as a prisoner of war.

It was Christmas Eve that someone told him a nineteen-year-old

American prisoner down the hall was badly depressed and possibly suicidal. Miller decided to pay the man a visit.

To break the ice, he mentioned the POW band he'd started, with the help of the Red Cross. The young man, he learned, played saxophone. The two began to exchange details about their families. Was he married, the kid asked? "Yeah, since '38," responded Miller.

"Have you got her picture?" the soldier asked. So Miller reached for his wallet, and pulled out a photograph of his wife.

"She's beautiful!" the young man responded. Then he noticed that a second picture had fallen out, and an expression of wonder crossed his face. "Where did you get that?" Miller told the story of the waitress at the California hamburger stand.

"That's my fiancé," the incredulous man said. Miller kept his promise to the beautiful girl back home and turned the picture over to its rightful owner.

The men stayed in touch briefly, and then went their separate ways for the remaining months of the war. Miller and his wife settled in Florida. And what became of the young man who had thought to end his life? He married the woman in the photo.

Editor's note: This story ran on Christmas Eve, fifty years later. Clair Miller still calls it "my Christmas miracle."

MY TURN

★ ★ ★

LIEUTENANT COLONEL TOM D. BARNA,
DEPLOYED TO IRAQI FREEDOM

Dear son,

Right up front, let me tell you that I love you, I am proud of you, and I am safe. It's hard to believe I am over here again! When I left the desert ten years ago at the conclusion of the Gulf War, I just never thought I would be here again. When I was here last time, I was an active duty captain in the Marine Corps. This time I return as a lieutenant colonel in the Marine Corps Reserve.

I've joked with your mom about not being sure which was worse—leaving her alone with three babies (during the Gulf War) or leaving her behind with three teenagers. I can still hear her laughing.

Son, my deployment seems a little more personal this time. As you know, it was our nation that was attacked. It was our people who died. And this fire has been brewing for quite a while. I think all Americans are finally ready to rid the world of men bent on imposing their evil will. This time it's different; this time we just won't take it. This time we finish the fight.

I will be honest with you: Nothing in my life is greater than serving the Corps, God, and country. But I am here for another reason too—a reason that personally motivates me. I am here so you won't one day have to come back and finish something we didn't take care of here and now.

Your grandpa served in Korea and in Southeast Asia and is buried at Arlington National Cemetery. He fought so that I could live in a world of peace. Men and women like him ended the Cold War. Now it's my turn, along with men and women of my time. We must be at war, to once and for all bring a time where our children—that's you, Alex—can live in a world of real peace.

This one is for you!

I so very much miss you, your sisters, and your mom. I'll be home soon. We'll all be home soon. In the meantime, I will pray for you and dream of you often.

Love,

Dad

~

The heart of every child beats
to the rhythm of a father's love.

STEVE CURLEY

LOST AND FOUND

$\bigstar\ \bigstar\ \bigstar$

DAVID B. COLEMAN, NC1(SW),
UNITED STATES NAVY (RETIRED)

Family separation is an unfortunate necessity for those who go to sea. Their work and duty schedule keeps them busy night and day, helping to keep their minds focused on their jobs. Still, when the important family days on the calendar come along, it is difficult to quiet the pangs of the heart.

One of my tours of duty found me stationed aboard a ship homeported out of Yokosuka, Japan. The ship was the USS *Mobile Bay* (CG-53), a Ticonderoga-class Aegis guided missile cruiser. My wife and our two boys lived in Japan while I was at sea for most of my three-year tour there. On one of the many deployments I spent with the *Mobile Bay*, our schedule had been very busy and mail was slow getting to us. We had been away from our home port for nearly six months, and it would be another two months before we returned to Yokosuka. My wife's birthday had come and gone, and our anniversary was rapidly approaching. It was hard not to think about her and our boys. Then the strangest thing happened. The ship crossed the International Date Line and the calendar jumped one day from June 28 to June 30. Our anniversary had vanished!

Some men forget their anniversary, but now I had lost the thing altogether. The ship had a policy of giving the men onboard a nice dinner on their birthdays and anniversaries, taking some of the sting out of having to be away for those occasions. Now, not only was I not spending our anniversary with my wife, but I had lost out on a nice dinner, too.

My friends asked me why I was so down. I explained my situation, and, in a typical response from sailors, they all laughed. I had to smile at the irony in it. They helped me by listening and letting me talk about my family.

The next morning, as I was making my way to the office, I noticed some handwritten signs taped to the bulkheads along the way. They read, "Lost, one 12th Wedding Anniversary. If found, please contact NC1(SW) Coleman at extension—." I went through a multitude of emotions. The guys on board greeted me that morning with, "Hey NC1, how ya' doin'?" And, "If I find your anniversary, I'll let you know ASAP!"

When I got to my office, the chaplain was taping a similar sign to our office door. As the command career counselor, I shared an office with him. He put his hand on my shoulder and said, "God works in mysterious ways." He grinned as we went inside.

The rest of the morning came and went without much incident. Then, that afternoon, I received a call from the commanding officer to report to his cabin. I hustled it up to his cabin and knocked on the door three times. As I opened the door I saw him holding one of the many signs that my shipmates had posted on my behalf. He asked how I was doing, and if there was anything he could do to help me retrieve my lost anniversary.

I was feeling really embarrassed now. I smiled, felt my cheeks burning a bit, and said, "No, thank you, sir, nothing I can think of."

He smiled at me. "There's a phone call for you." He handed me his phone.

"Hello?" The voice on the other end was my wife! We had our first conversation in over three months and it was wonderful. We talked for a few minutes, I said a quick hello to both of my sons, and told my wife I loved her as we said good-bye.

I handed the phone back to the CO and he said to report to the galley and see the chief there because he had something for me. I said I would, thanked him for that wonderful gift, and then headed below to the mess decks. When I got there, the chow line had already formed, but the chief took me to the head of the line where his staff had prepared a nice anniversary dinner for me. Everyone was smiling and wishing me well. It was a wonderful dinner, even though I could hardly swallow for the knot in my throat.

I met some amazing and talented people during my navy career. But without a doubt, the men on the *Mobile Bay* were the brightest and the best. They understood my burden, and with a little good-natured navy humor and lots of caring, they helped me through it in the best of ways.

The chaplain was right. God does work in mysterious ways. Had I not lost our anniversary, I would not have found that special camaraderie with shipmates nor had the wonderful experience of the phone call from home.

HE IS GONE

★★★

ELLIE KAY

I remember the morning I took my husband to deploy for Red Flag. From this exercise on the West Coast, they faced the possibility of going to the Middle East. There weren't enough jets to go around, so some pilots had gathered at the squadron to be bussed to the airport for commercial travel.

The sky was overcast that morning while the sun played peek-a-boo with the clouds. As Bob and I drove to the rendezvous point, I was already transitioning into the "take charge so I can cope" mode that most military wives have to switch to. I told Bob to slow down, informed him he needed to change lanes, and reminded him to change his underwear every night.

We pulled up to the squadron and Bob walked to the back of the Suburban to unload his gear. They were required to put their g-suits, survival gear, and flight suits into luggage. The F-117 Stealth pilots hand carried their helmets as their only allowable piece of carry on baggage. I would have given just about anything to see those dozen pilots walking through the airport concourse with conspicuously similar round green bags, looking like part of military bowling team!

After Bob put his gear in a pile with the other guys' stuff, it was time to quickly tell the World's Greatest Fighter Pilot good-bye. As I hugged my handsome aging warrior, I was keenly aware of the fact that we could be saying good-bye for two weeks, two months, and briefly, ever so briefly, the thought came that it could even be forever.

I fought back that thought even as I fought back the tears. Bob whispered in my ear, "The Lord bless you and keep you. The Lord make His face to shine upon you and give you peace." At that moment, the sun broke through the clouds and shown down upon my upturned face, resting on Bob's shoulder.

Together or apart, God will make His face to shine upon His servants. And He has given me peace.

A SOLDIER'S LEGACY

★ ★ ★

RON GOLD
RETOLD FROM A NEWSPAPER STORY

I was only seventeen when Grandma Elsie died. She was my last living grandparent and I was her only grandchild. Until the lawyer read her will, I never fully appreciated the depth of the woman's love.

It was a moment I will never forget. Mom, Dad, Aunt Sophie, Uncle Bill, and I sat around a small conference table in her attorney's office. She wanted her daughters and their husbands to share what little monetary wealth she left: the proceeds of her small insurance policy, an antique cameo, a few bracelets, some costume jewelry, and her wedding band. She also bequeathed them the deed to her house, her bank account, a few shares of stock in the local gas and electric company, and the American flag she was presented at Grandpa Edwin's military funeral.

Then, as we rose to leave, the attorney said, "There are three more things." He reached into his briefcase and brought out a small jewelry box, a letter, and a stack of envelopes neatly wrapped in tissue paper and tied with a fading pink ribbon.

"Jeffrey, your grandmother left you her diamond engagement ring, hoping you'll make good use of it soon."

Everyone smiled.

"These are also for you, Jeffrey," he said. "It may be the most valuable legacy of all—a letter and this stack of love notes."

This was Grandma's letter:

Dear Jeffrey,

I am leaving you one of my most precious treasures—my memories. These memories are the letters your Grandfather Edwin wrote when he was away from me. Please read them. They are both priceless and valuable; a guidebook that will teach you how to love a woman and how to understand people and how to respect and maintain your integrity. When you read them you will share the longing and passion a good man feels for a good woman—and you will also discover the empowering enchantment they will give you.

You will also understand the fears and tears of war. And you will realize the differences between right and wrong. You will learn to trust the people you love and keep your distance from those you mistrust. You will learn about mature friendships and how true love can become the core of your life.

I have been fortunate, Jeffrey. I loved a wonderful man. And he loved me. While his love is now a memory, it is also a real dream that never ends. Love is like a beautiful photograph you store in an album. You can enjoy its beauty each time you stare at its wonderment. It stops time. And it makes you young again—forever!

Grandpa Edwin was a soldier, a professional army officer who chased Pancho Villa back to Mexico with John J. Pershing. He also served under General Pershing in the trenches in France during World War I.

To understand your grandfather's soul, read his loving letters to me. You'll learn how romantic and beautiful a real man can be. To understand Grandpa's character, read the personal note Jack Pershing wrote me when he heard that Edwin was killed in action.

Jeffrey, I said this packet of notes was priceless and valuable. I've just shown you how priceless his love notes are. Please learn from them. Then find the right girl to love and love her ardently. This love will enrich both your lives and make you both happier.

As for being valuable, save the envelopes. An appraiser at Sotheby's said the old stamps are worth far more than the rest of my estate. And the handwritten note from General Pershing is even more valuable than the stamps.

Have a loving, bountiful life. God bless you.

I love you,

Grandma Elsie

A Letter Home

✦ ✦ ✦

6 July 1966

Dear Ginger,

Not one thing has changed here since I wrote yesterday. I guess I just feel like talking to you...

The pain of being away from you is very real. It brings home to my heart how strong, real, and full our love is. I pray continually for God to be with us through this to a blessed reunion.

With all my love,

Frank

EXCERPT FROM A LETTER SENT FROM CAPTAIN FRANK COFFMAN TO HIS WIFE SHORTLY AFTER ARRIVING IN VIETNAM

STILL, SMALL VOICE

★★★

Robert L. Hilton

God always gives us what we need when we need it. One night in 1969, God gave me courage just when I needed it. It came as a tiny voice from thousands of miles away, and it embedded deep within my heart.

In 1968 and 1969, I was stationed near Ho Phat, Vietnam, near the Da Nang airbase. I was a gunnery sergeant with the 1st Marine Air Wing and worked as a noncommissioned officer in charge of the ground radio repair shop.

Seventeen thousand miles away my wife, Akiko, raised our five children at home in Barstow, California. She and I wrote frequent letters to each other, but every once in a while she surprised me with an audiocassette tape so I could play and replay my family's voices.

On that day in 1969, I'd gotten one of those rare tapes from Akiko at mail call. She spoke first, and then one by one our children talked to their daddy. They talked like all kids talk to a tape recorder—speaking in that kid-slurry way, breathing into the microphone, and filling the pauses with sighs and silence.

The last to talk was Kimberly, our four-year-old daughter. Because she was the last, she didn't get much space on that tape. Kimberly was the youngest girl, and I imagined her big sister and three brothers elbowing her to the end of the line. She said, "Hello, Daddy. Daddy, when are you coming home?" And then the tape ran out. That's all I heard of my little daughter.

The barracks I slept in had been built without partitions—only four walls and a roof—and awhile earlier we'd traded some steaks for plywood to make individual rooms. In my small bedroom, I'd put my bunk up on stilts, creating a two-and-a-half-foot crawl space for protection against shrapnel in case we came under attack.

I would need that protection that night, because earlier in the day we'd heard of a possible enemy assault. Before I went to bed, I cleaned my .45-caliber pistol, wiped down the bullets, and hung my gas mask on the plywood wall beside my bed. Then I put my helmet near the head of the bed and the weapon under my pillow. I planned out my course of action: In one quick, graceful sweep, I'd put on my flak jacket, snatch my gas mask from the wall, grab my helmet and weapon, and roll under the bed. I was ready for anything.

As always before going to sleep, I prayed for my family. I knew Akiko was having a difficult time at home alone with the kids. I also prayed for my own protection and, as always, submitted myself to His care.

Close to midnight the first rocket whistled in. When you hear that whistle, you can practically see the rocket in your mind, sailing in as you wait for the explosion and then the spray of shrapnel and debris.

I heard the whistle, and in slow motion I imagined that rocket coming into my barracks and crashing. It hit somewhere outside the barracks. Then I heard the machine gun's rapid fire with it. I heard the shrapnel hit. I don't remember any movements from that point, but things happened so fast. When that first one exploded, I found myself under the bed on the concrete floor, and I realized that all the preparation I had made at bedtime was still in its place. I had no gas mask, helmet, and no weapon to protect me.

Rockets usually came in twos, and as I lay on the floor waiting for the second one to hit, I feared that I wasn't going to make it. Then, somewhere in all that chaos and panic, I heard the thin, clear voice of my daughter: "Daddy, when are you coming home?" It repeated over and over in my head. My daughter called. She needed me to stay alive.

I got the strength of courage then. I had to make it—I would make it. I thought only of that child because it was the last voice I'd heard on the tape. And because it was—though brief—the voice I needed to hear.

~

Love
always protects,
always trusts,
always hopes,
always perseveres.

FROM THE BIBLE
1 CORINTHIANS 13:7

A FATHER'S LEGACY TO HIS DAUGHTER

MAJOR SARAH A. MCMULLEN
AS TOLD TO CHARLOTTE ADELSPERGER

I n my sophomore year of college, I volunteered to instruct cross-country skiing for my college's ROTC winter lab at what I thought was "Camp McCoy" in Wisconsin.

When I told Dad, he chuckled. "You mean *Fort* McCoy. That's where I did National Guard service. Cold as Greenland!"

As it turned out my experience there was such fun, I thought the army life might be for me. So I signed up for the summer boot camp at Fort Knox, Kentucky. What a rude awakening! It was horribly lonely, physically demanding, and mentally draining.

I phoned my parents, sobbing. "This is too hard! I can't handle it!" They let me pour it all out. Then I heard their voices filled with caring and affirmation.

"Hang in there, Sarah," Dad told me. "It takes fortitude and faith to face training. I know from experience—and I know what you're made of."

Immediately I imagined scenes of Dad in uniform—and his years of perseverance wearing it. Known as Staff Sergeant Kenneth M. Hodges, Wisconsin National Guard, he was now my cheerleader.

While at boot camp I ached for time with Dad, who understood the rigors I encountered every day. He was a peaceful, reserved man with kind eyes. He showed strong Christian faith and attended church regularly. My mind shifted back to those late night talks around the kitchen table, him in his chair and me in mine, always across from each other. He would be there grinning—a nonverbal invitation to sit and talk in the darkened house lit only by the kitchen light. My mom worked third shift at the hospital, so this was our time together. When our sharing ended, he would always say, "You're one of the best" and rub my head as he walked by my chair.

The next two years of ROTC were extremely challenging, a period of personal growth. The training was intense, sometimes more mentally than physically. The army changed me—it made me more equipped as a person, more sure of who I was.

One of my proudest military moments was accepting my commission as an army officer on May 15, 1988. My mom and dad, one on each side, pinned on my second lieutenant bars. I can still see Mom glowing and Dad in his blue suit, smiling so proudly. I felt like one of the best!

I moved to South Carolina, and there I met Scott McMullen, my future husband. By then I was a first lieutenant.

The night before our wedding, I was in my parents' home. The kitchen light was still on, and I knew where I needed to be. There was a father waiting up to chat one last time with his only daughter. We talked again about my military service as an important opportunity to serve my country.

On his way to turn off the lights, he said, "You're one of the best" and rubbed my head.

During our fourth year of marriage, my dad fell gravely ill with cancer. During his six-month battle with the disease, I had a chance to meet him for one last late-night discussion to glean all that I could about love, life, and the meaning of it all. Across the table we shared stories. I told him I was thankful for everything he had done, and for encouraging me to stay the course.

Five weeks after our son Connor was born, I got the urgent call that Dad was failing. I made it home in time for one final embrace, and to look into Dad's kind eyes for the last time. I thanked God that he allowed my father to meet his new grandson.

Dad was failing. I made it home in time for one final embrace, and to look into Dad's kind eyes for the last time. I thanked God that he allowed my father to meet his new grandson.

In 2002 I was promoted to major. At my pinning ceremony my husband Scott and son Connor stood one at each shoulder. Our toddler Sophie watched eagerly. When I gave my remarks, I thanked Scott, who helps me through extremely difficult juggling of family, work, and army. And of course, I spoke of my dad as thoughts of him flooded my mind.

When I retire, I plan to mount my discharge certificate below my father's. Often I ponder about the combination of human spirit and God's love that was my dad. I think of the legacy he left me of faith, patriotism, and unconditional love. I think of women and men in the U.S. military all over the world. Oh, how I hope someone is telling them, "You're one of the best."

THE ROSE

$$\bigstar \; \bigstar \; \bigstar$$

JENNIFER SHERWOOD
AS TOLD TO BEDELIA BURCHETTE MURRAY

Jennifer stared at the framed rose and smiled. She couldn't help it.

To look at the framed rose upon her wall always brightened her face because it reminded her heart that she was precious to her husband. To others he may be a Special Forces Green Beret, but to her, this tough guy was the special man who would search all over a foreign land for her favorite flower. Just looking at it now brought back the memories…

During the months that Jennifer and Sergeant Kevin Sherwood had dated, he had continually showered her with hand-picked roses, and when those were not in season he arranged to have them sent to her from a florist.

Then, in October 1990, Kevin was deployed to the Gulf for Operation Desert Storm. Kevin was still in the Middle East during February 1991, and though Jennifer didn't expect flowers or candy for Valentine's Day, she secretly hoped for a card.

Nothing arrived on Valentine's Day.

But a few days later something did.

In the mailbox was a large envelope from Kevin. Inside were a letter and a wad of tissue paper. In the letter he wrote:

I want to let you know this; you are a rarer find than a flower in the desert. 'Like a lily among the thorns, so is my darling among the maidens' (Song of Songs 2:2). I'm no poet, writer, speaker, or singer, but I love you.

Unwrapping the tissue paper, she found the most beautiful dried long-stemmed red rose, her favorite.

It would be a few days later before Kevin called. "You wouldn't believe what it took to find a red rose out here. It seemed like I found the only one in the entire country!"

At that moment, Jennifer knew he was the man with whom she wanted to spend the rest of her life.

Nine years later the rose, now framed, still hangs on the wall. They now have two children and feel blessed that their love has only gotten stronger over the years.

Kevin is again deployed overseas. But Jennifer knows the peace that comes with trusting God to do what's best and is thankful that God is with her husband. And she is thankful for the rose and how much Kevin loves her. She is proud to be his wife and grateful that he is serving our country.

To Lucasta

★★★

GOING TO THE WARS

Tell me not, Sweet, I am unkind,
That from the nunnery
Of thy chaste breast and quiet mind
To war and arms I fly.
True, a new mistress now I chase,
The first foe in the field;
And with a stronger faith embrace
A sword, a horse, a shield.
Yet this inconstancy is such
As thou too shalt adore;
I could not love thee, Dear so much,
Loved I not Honor more.

RICHARD LOVELACE

MEETING FATHER

★ ★ ★

LAURA TINDAL HULETT
AS TOLD TO LAUREN THOMPSON,
HER SEVENTEEN-YEAR-OLD GRANDDAUGHTER

Five-year-old Laura Tindal was awakened by the crash of the lamp shattering on the floor of her bedroom. She sat up, bleary-eyed, and tried to figure out what had made it fall.

That's when she heard it.

A menacing rumble shook the house, and the roar of engines outside her window made her clamp her hands over her ears. She was used to hearing planes pass over the house—they lived on the Army Air Corps base at Hickam Field, Hawaii. Practice flights went on at all hours of the day and night. But this morning it sounded like the entire Army Air Corps was landing in her backyard. The early light filtered through the shades drawn over her bedroom window. Laura stretched. It was Sunday, December 7. The year was 1941.

She wasn't particularly afraid, only upset about the broken lamp, which was her favorite. She ambled into the room of her parents, Major Lorry Tindal and Laura Tindal, intending to wake them up and ask what all the noise was outside. They were already up and dressing hurriedly. As soon as Laura's mother finished dressing, she hastily put on Laura's clothes and told her and her older sister to go hide in the butler's pantry. As Laura ran to the pantry, she looked around for her father and realized he was already gone. The sound of the aircraft was still there, but was now being joined by something else—a pounding sound that shook the earth, as if dinosaurs were dancing down their driveway.

Laura's mother dashed around the house opening all the windows to prevent them from being shattered by the force of the explosions. Then, from inside the pantry Laura heard a deafening crash. An aircraft had fallen to the ground right outside their window, just missing the house. Mrs. Tindal uttered a terrified scream and hurried into the pantry with her daughters.

One by one, other houses on the street were bombed, and women and children fled to the Tindal house and scrambled to hide underneath the dining table, piano, and any other shelter they could find. They stayed there, waiting with a horrifying realization that they might not come out of it alive. Several hours later, when the attack finally ended, Laura and her mother bundled into the car of a friend and evacuated to Honolulu with the rest of the military families.

It wasn't until five years later that a knock came on the door of the apartment where Laura and her mother had lived ever since the Japanese attack that thrust America into the war. When Mrs. Tindal answered the door, she burst out in tears. Laura, now age ten, walked into the room to see what all the excitement was about. She saw her mother crying in the arms of a tall man in uniform. As she came into the room, her mother released her tight embrace and tried to dry her tears. The man walked up to Laura and extended his hand to shake hers.

"Hello, Laura, I'm your father, Lorry Tindal."

Laura felt excitement, joy, shock, and disbelief all at once. She had nearly forgotten what he looked like. He had sent letters, but only every so often and always marked up by the mail censors. Now he was standing here in front of her, and she had no idea what to say to him.

Her father broke the awkward silence. "Would you like to go out and have a party to celebrate our reunion?"

"Yes, sir," was all she could muster. Inside, Laura was relieved and happy, but it would be awhile before she would be comfortable calling him "daddy" again.

On September 11, 2001, I watched our country being attacked on live television. I live in Maryland, near the Pentagon, and the uncertainty that descended on our community gave me a new appreciation for the stories about Pearl Harbor that I've heard from my grandmother, Laura Tindal. She often talked about how hard it was growing up with her daddy gone for five years. During World War II, hundreds of thousands of servicemen left their families behind and often did not see them again for years. While they were gone, their only communication was through letters and an occasional telegram. When they returned home, the horrors that they witnessed in battle were seldom discussed.

Today, we are again sending servicemen and women overseas to fight in a new war against a new evil. Our brave military personnel are feeling the pain that distance from one's family brings. I am proud of those who put themselves in harm's way in order to safeguard our way of life and free others from oppression.

I'm glad for e-mail and satellite phones that enable soldiers to stay closer to their loved ones, because perhaps that closeness serves to remind them of why they are there. My grandmother and I talk on the phone often, and she thinks that the images of liberation that we see on the television should remind us of the necessity to stand up for what's right.

We should be thankful to everyone who serves because of all they have done for this country.

FOR OTHERS FIRST

$$\star \; \star \; \star$$

Scott Buckingham
Air Force Tech Sergeant,
deployed to Middle East

Dear Kyle,

Happy eleventh birthday! I really miss your smiling face and happy laugh. Are you shoveling the driveway? I hope so. Mom needs your help right now because you're the man there.

Let's talk about being a man. I think you're old enough to understand. Being a man isn't about being big, or smart, or strong, or tough. Being a man means knowing that your life is over. What I mean by that is a man does stuff for others first and for himself last. I learned that the day you were born, and that was the greatest day of my life. I had an equally great day when Kayleigh was born.

Almost everything I do is for you, or your sister, or your mom. If you guys are safe and happy, then I'm happy. That's why I go to work, so we can have the things we need and some of the things we want. That's why I get mad when you don't do well in school, because doing well in school almost guarantees doing well in life. And that's why I hug you every day, because if you hug me back then I know I'm doing a pretty good job. So it may be your birthday, but it's an anniversary for me too. Take care and stay special.

Love,

Dad

P.S. You don't need to become a man right away. It took me thirty years. You can at least wait until you're twelve.

OUR CHRISTMAS TREE

★ ★ ★

Irene Costilow

I
t was Christmas 1970 and I hoped our poor, pathetic tree would survive for Pete's homecoming. We were postponing our celebration until his return home from the war in Vietnam. He was "short"—which meant less than thirty days left in country. Daily we marked the days off the calendar—January 18 was *the* day.

Our poor tree was getting drier by the minute with pine needles all over the floor. It was a humorous sight with the ornaments strewn about. We didn't dare turn the lights on for fear the tree would catch on fire. But I was determined to keep that tree up until Pete came home and we would have Christmas together. Could that tree make it just a few more days?

Oh, Lord, please bring him home safely became my constant prayer. He had flown every single day of the past year as a U.S. Army helicopter pilot. My biggest fear was that his last flight in the country might possibly be his last and he wouldn't make it home.

David was five months old when his daddy left. He thought *Daddy* was the Chinook helicopters that flew over our house near Fort Sill, Oklahoma. That was the helicopter that Pete flew in Vietnam. When we would see one, I would say to David, "See, that's what Dada flies. See Dada?" I guess I didn't explain it well enough. But our little seventeen-month-old was eagerly awaiting the day when all those gifts under the tree could be opened with his daddy.

The day finally arrived! We ran into his arms at the Oklahoma City airport. But David was terrified of him. I felt so badly for Pete because it broke his heart. I encouraged him to just be patient and eventually David would warm up to him. It didn't take too long! David was fascinated with the medals on Pete's uniform. He would touch them with his little fingers, look at his daddy, and with the sweetest expression on his face, say "Mine, mine?" I'll never forget the sheer joy on Pete's face as his little boy became his best buddy.

We drove back to our home and walked in the door to our pathetic little Christmas tree. Pete just burst into laughter. He couldn't stop laughing. Of course, it was wonderful to hear that laugh of his again. When he finally stopped laughing, he took me in his arms and said "Merry Christmas forever!" We had our belated Christmas and it was the most beautiful Christmas we could ever ask for.

What a joyful reunion! Pete was home—all in one piece. God had answered my prayers. My twenty-four-year-old soldier husband had bravely served his country by fighting a war that was bitterly opposed by so many. He had faced death and been exposed to things that no one should have to ever see, especially someone that young. His heart was full of gratitude to have made it home; so many of his buddies didn't. And he was proud to have served his country. I was proud of him too.

Today my husband is still a soldier. He serves in the Oklahoma Army National Guard. He is older, wiser, and still incredibly proud to serve the best country in the world. His eyes fill with tears when he has to send other young soldiers into harm's way. His heart breaks as he watches them say good-bye to their young wives and precious children. Memories flood his mind of that time he spent away from his family, not knowing whether he would ever see them again.

Many years have passed since that day long ago, but every Christmas we reminisce and say a prayer of thanksgiving for Pete's safe return home.

It was a Christmas we will always cherish as the three of us celebrated by remembering the birth of Jesus and the gift of eternal life we have been given through His sacrifice on a tree.

Author's note: My husband is brigadier general in the Oklahoma Army National Guard, serving as the assistant adjutant general for Oklahoma. He is also the first army aviator in Oklahoma to make brigadier general. Our family grew into three sons: David is thirty-four, married and has two little girls; and our twin sons, Kelly and Kevin, are thirty. We are extremely blessed! We have the opportunity to speak for Stonecroft Ministries, sharing our story of God's grace in dealing with the diagnosis that our twin sons are mentally handicapped.

He dreams, he plans.
He struggles that we might have the best.
His sacrifice is quiet, his life is love expressed.

AUTHOR UNKNOWN

WELCOME HOME

★★★

ALICE GRAY

First Troops Returning from Iraqi Freedom

With flags, banners, and balloons waving, hundreds of families shout and cheer as two navy missile cruisers return from Iraq. They left ten months ago and now the sailors serving on the USS *Shiloh* and USS *Mobile Bay* are home.

Private boats and other navy vessels sound their horns in greeting. One signalman aboard the docked USS *Coronado* flashes, "welcome home," and the USS *Shiloh* flashes back, "glad to be home."

One little girl with small flags tied to her braids jumps up and down shouting, "Daddy, Daddy." A white navy hat perches on the head of a five-year-old boy as he waits with his hand on his forehead in proud salute. A few steps away, a young mother holds a newborn baby who sleeps contentedly in a tiny navy uniform. With tear-stained cheeks and broad smiles, parents, wives, and husbands scan the decks for their loved ones.

The captain decides that the first eighteen men to step off the USS *Shiloh* will be new fathers—sailors whose sons and daughters were born while they were gone. Wives wrap their husbands in tearful embraces and then step back and watch as babies and daddies reach for one another.

As long as there are freedoms to defend, scenes like this will be repeated time and time again as men and women of the United States military come home from afar.

We will not forget the men and women who will stay in Iraq helping that nation to prosper and helping the people discover what freedom means. And we will never, ever forget those who gave their lives in Operation Iraqi Freedom. Nor will we forget their loved ones.

But there is a time to weep and a time to dance. And as our troops come home, it is a time to dance. Welcome home you men and women who have represented our country so well. We are thankful. We are proud.

INSPIRATION

ALWAYS FREE

We will always remember.
We will always be proud.
We will always be prepared,
so we may always be free.

PRESIDENT RONALD REAGAN

THE PRAYER CARD

$$\bigstar\ \bigstar\ \bigstar$$

CHARLOTTE ADELSPERGER

Day after day for many weeks Joe, age twenty-two, agonized through grueling challenges at army boot camp in Fort Knox, Kentucky. Even though proud to be in the United States military, he was sometimes so exhausted, he wondered if he'd make it through training. He drew on his closeness to God, savored his mother's letters, and dreamed of marrying his sweetheart Tara.

His mom, Suzy, often responded to the discouragement in his letters with "Be strong in the Lord" or "Go for the gold—you can do it."

One day Joe wrote about how the men all lined up and were each assigned a partner or "battle buddy." "We need to know everything about our buddy down to his shoe size," he commented. "We're trained to look after each other wherever we go."

Joe liked his buddy Anthony right off. They began to share everything and cheer each other on. Both were Christians—Anthony, Roman Catholic; Joe, Protestant. Many nights throughout boot camp some of the guys would gather in the barracks for prayer and sharing. Joe and Anthony, with their Bibles in hand, would lead the group.

One day Anthony got a worn-out prayer card in the mail from his mother. On one side was a line drawing of head and shoulders of Jesus.

His likeness showed strength and hope. On the other side was a simple prayer for protection Anthony prayed with the group almost every night.

His mom had written in her note, "You pray this prayer and God will get you through anything."

Sometimes when the group was feeling down, Anthony would hold up the card. "Come on guys, we can make it through. We've got the good Lord watching our backs."

Joe remembered those words and treasured each evening with the group. He lived close to God, deeply cared about others, and saw service to his country as one of God's callings.

When Joe's parents, Mike and Suzy, attended his graduation at boot camp, Joe took them to meet Anthony. "This is my battle buddy—you've got to meet him!"

Suzy gave Anthony a big hug. "I've heard what a special friend you are. I'm so glad you guys were here for each other."

Mike smiled as he shook Anthony's hand.

But sadness hovered over the two buddies who had become like brothers. Anthony would be leaving for more army training in Fort Bliss, Texas. Joe would go to Fort Hood, Texas, for training to be a cavalry scout.

"Well, one of these days we'll be separated," Anthony said. He drew a breath. "But it looks like we're both going to the Middle East." His eyes moistened as he reached into his pocket. "The prayer card is now yours." He slipped it into Joe's hand.

"Thanks," Joe said, looking down at the card. He shuffled his feet, and then pointed to the picture. "That'll be the tattoo on my back!" Everyone chuckled.

During his ten-day leave, Joe and Tara were married. Then before going to Fort Hood, they went to see Joe's parents.

One day when his mom came home from work, Joe greeted her. "Mom, I have to show you something." He pulled off his shirt. A thin plastic covering clung to his slim back. When she saw traces of blood across his dark skin, a chill swept over her. There beneath the plastic bandage was the very sketch of Jesus that had been on the prayer card—about six inches high between the shoulder blades of her son.

"Oh my word! You really did it!" She fought tears as she pictured Joe with this image on his back on the front lines of a battlefield.

"You don't get a tattoo just for the fun of it. I prayed about this one. Now wherever I go in life, it'll be a reminder who's with me."

Weeks later Private First Class Joe, a recipient of honors, was deployed with U.S. Army troops to the Middle East where he valiantly served on the front lines during Operation Iraqi Freedom.

But before Joe left, he wrote his mom. "You know, when guys see Jesus right there on my skin, I tell 'em, 'The Lord's watching my back—and yours too.' It helps us all be stronger."

THE PHOTO THAT ANSWERED A PRAYER

Andrew Knox
for *CWNews*
April 11, 2003

When is a picture worth more than a thousand words? Ask the parents of a marine sergeant involved in the Iraq war. For them, a combat photo and a battlefront letter proved that God hears our prayers.

The image of Marine Sergeant Jesse Lanter carrying an injured fellow marine off the battlefield—it's one of the most powerful and widely seen images in the war with Iraq, so far. It displayed the loyalty of members of the 1st Marine Division as they came under fire from Iraqi troops.

But as the hero's father and stepmother David and Alyson Lanter explained, it also means much more.

Alyson said, "To the world, they view him as a war hero. We're not saying he isn't, but to us he was a hero before that picture. To us he's always been a hero. To us that picture is an answer to prayer."

David and Alyson knew Jesse was somewhere in Iraq, most likely on the frontline advance to Baghdad. But the news they were seeing on television wasn't good.

David said, "At the point that they started their advance and the marines started getting hurt or captured or killed, we really didn't know where he was. We didn't know his status. We didn't know if he was safe or not."

David added, "That was our prayer, to make sure he was okay and to know where he was." They prayed, "God, just please point him out, one time."

Soon after, newspapers across the country carried the famous photograph of their son Jesse rescuing Corporal Barry Lange at a standoff in Al Bayer, near Basra.

Alyson said, "We didn't know where he was or if he was alive. When we saw that picture—to us it was God answering our prayers! God saying 'here's your boy, he's in My hands, and he's gonna come home okay.'"

David said, "And in the print under the picture, to be able to read where he was, and see it in print, and to be able to follow him from there on out. That was the second answer, to me."

That was their second answered prayer concerning Jesse. Their first prayer had been answered soon after the war began.

Alyson said, "We had filled out a prayer request and put it on the altar of our church during our forty days of prayer and fasting. And the very first prayer request on there was for Jesse's salvation. He wrote us a letter and it said, 'So you don't worry, I've read the books you gave me, and I've taken Christ as my Savior.' When we got that letter, we both started crying."

Alyson added, "We just want to give God the glory for saving Jesse's soul! Of course we're still worried about him being over there and fighting in the war, but at the same time a huge burden was lifted, because we know that he's in God's hands."

Jesse's parents continue to pray for their son and all those on the battlefront who are putting their lives on the line, and our military wherever they are.

GRATEFUL WARRIOR

★★★

CHUCK HOLTON
FORMER U.S. ARMY RANGER

A light breeze filters through the maples shading the parking lot of the University of Virginia satellite clinic in the small town of Middlebrook. It's a warm day, but not uncomfortably so. In the distance, farmers are baling up the season's first cutting of hay. The tiny medical center sits on a hill overlooking rolling farmland, right next to the volunteer fire station for this village of about two hundred.

The eclectic decor inside the center's cramped office includes swords, photos from distant war zones, and a life-sized skeleton wearing a necktie. Then the doctor walks in, and it is obvious that the skeleton probably wears the tie more than he does.

Besides the neckwear, there's something else about Dr. Marsh that's clearly missing: an inflated ego.

"Call me Rob," he insists.

Nothing about the lanky man in blue jeans would suggest that he is one of the most decorated U.S. military physicians alive today.

"Let's go make some house calls," he says. "I'll drive."

Winding through green farmland in a dusty pickup truck, the doctor begins to share his testimony. As he looks back on his forty-seven years, it's easy to see God's hand in his life.

When Rob Marsh was young, he was uncertain of what he wanted to do. So in 1976, he went to speak to a recruiter about joining the special forces. The only slot available was that of a medic, so Marsh took it and enlisted. Over the next sixteen months, God blessed his efforts in the grueling A-team training course. One of the requirements for completing it was to graduate successfully from Airborne school. In the third week, Marsh slightly fractured his foot. Lying on his bunk, he prayed that God would somehow allow him to finish the training. He told no one about his injury and was able to complete two more jumps in order to graduate. From there it was on to the medical portion of the class, where the intensive medical training struck a chord with Rob. He couldn't seem to get enough of it.

Rob Marsh had found his calling.

Marsh's first assignment was as a physician with a unit assigned to Fort Eustis, Virginia. While there he was recruited into the Special Forces Operational Detachment—Delta, more commonly known as Delta Force.

Marsh thrived in the unit's close-knit environment. He worked to make changes in the way that medical care was administered, bringing procedures up to date and putting a higher priority on caring for the soldiers' families. Sometimes his policies garnered opposition from other officers, but it was clear to him that he was where he was supposed to be.

In 1990, someone dropped out of the residency program at the University of Virginia, and he was given the slot. "That was a total God thing," he says. Three years later, having finished his residency in family medicine, he returned to Delta, just in time to be deployed to Somalia, where he ran the aid station.

On October 3, the day of the fateful mission when two Black Hawk helicopters were shot down, and news coverage showed American bodies being dragged through the streets of Mogadishu, Marsh's medical training was severely tested as he struggled for forty-eight hours to save the lives of his fellow soldiers.

At about 9 P.M. on October 6, he was standing next to his friend, Matt Rierson, with a group of men in front of the hangar. A mortar round fired from somewhere in the city dropped right into the middle of them.

Rierson absorbed much of the blast and was killed instantly. The man on the other side of Marsh was also seriously wounded, along with ten others. Marsh was blown backward and knocked unconscious.

When he came to, someone had cut the lights. Instinctively, he began crawling toward the aircraft hangar, about fifty feet away. There was a first-aid trunk just inside the door. He pulled himself toward it with his hands and elbows. He was nearly there when the blackness caught up with him again.

He came to with several medics crowded around him. They had put him in a pair of anti-shock trousers to keep his blood pressure up, and he quickly felt surprisingly alert. Then he was being hustled onto a helicopter for a short ride to the MASH unit at the American embassy. It was there that another surgeon came to look him over. Marsh now got to experience what it was like to be on the other side of the gurney.

As soon as the shock trousers were deflated, Marsh passed out. He barely remembers being put on an aircraft bound for Germany several days later, and the next time he woke up, he was in a hospital and his wife, Barbara, was there.

"She literally nursed me back to health," says Marsh.

Shrapnel had ripped through his abdomen and lacerated his iliac artery, and he ultimately received seventeen units of blood. Ironically, it was the massive transfusion that almost killed him. He developed DIC, a blood condition that is almost always fatal, and was soon hovering near death.

When word got back to Rob's friends and family, they called their small country church in the Shenandoah Valley. The church began a vigil to pray for his healing.

Miraculously, Marsh pulled through.

"I am absolutely convinced that those prayers kept me alive," Rob says confidently. "That church is a big part of the reason that we decided to move here after I retired. I feel like I was saved so that I could come back and minister to these people."

And minister he does. In addition to being the only general practitioner for miles around, Marsh serves as an elder in the church, cares for prisoners at the nearby penitentiary, and is a member of the volunteer fire department. On top of all of this, Rob strives to keep his family first. Six years ago he and Barbara purchased a historic farm where their four young home-schooled children share in the chores.

The contrast between this idyllic setting and the far-flung war zones in his past couldn't be more striking, but in a way, living here reminds him of his time with Delta. He is intimately familiar with the details of his patients' lives, a fact that often amazes the many medical students who travel to Middlebrook to intern with him. The many surgeries and the painful therapy have given him empathy for his patients that he couldn't have known otherwise.

Marsh doesn't want to be remembered just as a great doctor; he wants to be remembered for making a consistent investment in the lives of his children, his church, and his community. He also hopes that he can inspire other doctors to pursue their callings.

While crisscrossing the Shenandoah Valley to make house calls on the poor and elderly may be neither lucrative nor efficient, Rob Marsh has found joy in the niche that God has him in at this point in his life.

He is pursuing the purpose for which he was created.

MIRACLE AT SEA

★★★

DAVID HARDY

Dear family and friends,

Last night I was witness to a true miracle. Around 10 P.M., a B-1 bomber with a crew of four went down about a hundred miles north of Diego Garcia. One of the pilots was talking on his radio from a survival raft, so we knew that at least one had survived. It took us about an hour to race north as close as we could get to the crash site. They had gone down over a shallow bank, so our ship had to stand off about seven miles away.

We put the small boats in the water. As we headed away from the ship, there were three things I'll always remember—the eerie smell of jet fuel in the water, the magnificent number of stars in the sky, and a confidence that everything would be all right.

We didn't see the light until we were about a mile away and came upon two pilots sitting in their survival rafts. Right about the same time, we spotted another strobe. As we hauled them up into the boat, one of them greeted us calmly: "Hey guys, thanks for coming. It's good to see you."

The other boat picked up the third guy, and we were told to bring the three back to the ship. On the way, and just as we were about to pass him, the fourth pilot lit off his flare just long enough to be noticed, and we located him a couple of minutes later using night-vision goggles. He was the one who had been talking on his radio the whole time.

The pilots had ejected from their plane at 17,000 feet, upside down, falling at three hundred knots and had landed spread out in shallow water in the middle of nowhere. Our boats were guided right to the downed pilots. They were in rough shape but amazingly composed. By 2 A.M., four hours after the crash, all were onboard the USS *Russell*. It had to be a miracle. Finding that fourth pilot and being able to tell buddies that their whole crew was safe, was just about the best feeling in the whole world. That moment made all of this worthwhile. I wanted to share it.

Hope all's well with everyone at home.

God bless,

Dave

∾

*For those who fight for it,
freedom has a flavor the
protected will never know.*

WRITTEN ON A C-RATION BOX FOUND
AFTER THE SIEGE OF KHE SANH, 1968

A CIRCLE ON
THE CALENDAR

TECHNICAL SERGEANT HUGH ASBURY NEELY
AS TOLD TO CANDY NEELY ARRINGTON

The plane tilted precariously, nose-down. Smoke swirled around me as flames licked their way up one wing. The pilot's shout above the engine noise confirmed what I already knew—our plane was going to crash. I motioned for the tail gunner to jump. He gave a salute before disappearing into the black hole beyond the open doorway. One of the younger guys clutched the straps of his parachute with a white-knuckled hand. I saw the fear in his eyes.

"Hurry," I yelled.

Haltingly he moved toward the door, then stopped. The emergency light bathed his frightened face in an eerie glow.

"I can't!"

"You've got to, man. We're going down."

"No!"

I saw the panic rising in this recruit and did the only thing I could. I pushed him with all my might and prayed his chute would open. I counted mentally, then followed him into black nothingness.

As the wind struck my face, a sharp involuntary intake of air filled my lungs. I breathed a prayer. *Father, protect me.* I had no idea where I would land or what awaited me once on the ground. My life verse, given to me at birth by a missionary uncle, passed through my mind. "I can do all things through him who strengthens me" (Philippians 4:13). Could I? Did I really believe that, no matter what lay ahead?

The ground rose to meet me, jarring me so totally the landing knocked the breath from me. I needed to move quickly. Our flaming plane was a beacon to the enemy. Its explosion into the silent countryside screamed our presence. Quickly I gathered my parachute and pulled the harness straps from my shoulders. I saw movement to my left and ducked behind a haystack. It was the tail gunner.

"Which way should we go?" he asked.

"I was hoping you'd know. Let's get out of here. We're sitting ducks in this field."

We ran two hundred yards to the edge of the woods and disappeared under its protective canopy. A muffled hiss drew our eyes upward. There was the fellow I'd pushed, suspended from the towering branches. I made quick work of shimmying up the trunk and cutting him down. Indistinguishable shouts propelled us deeper into the woods. We were running now. The search dogs were not far behind. We ran until my frightened charge tripped on a gnarled root.

"I can't go on," he panted.

"Yes, you can," I insisted.

Jerking him to his feet we continued our uncharted course. Suddenly, a wire loomed before us.

"It's the border!" he cried, louder than was safe.

"Shhh...but *what* border?"

Indecision plagued us as the minutes dragged by. Again I prayed. *Father, we need Your direction. Show me the way.* Silently, the answer formed in my mind: *cross over.*

"Come on. We're going over," I said with a confidence I didn't really feel.

"But how can you be sure?"

"I can't be sure. I just have faith that it's the right thing to do."

We crossed the border into an unknown country and walked until we collapsed. I awoke to stare down a gun barrel. The soldiers pointing their guns at us spoke German, but it was Swiss-German. We had crossed into Switzerland, a neutral country. The days ahead meant internment, housed in an unheated hotel high in the Alps above Adelboden. God faithfully guided us out of Nazi-occupied territory and away from the concentration camps.

When I finally escaped through the underground seven months later and was sent home, I discovered what happened stateside when my plane went down.

My mother's eyes were continually drawn to the calendar. With three sons away at war, the nagging, unknowing pull to a specific date on the calendar gave her a sick feeling in the pit of her stomach. She tried to busy herself with household chores, but returned often to stand before the calendar. Finally, she picked up a pen and circled the date that wouldn't leave her alone.

At the lumberyard, my father sat in his office. Numerous details claimed his attention, but his eyes returned again and again to a certain date on the calendar. What did it mean? Why was that day significant? Finally, exasperated, he circled the date with a bold, red stroke.

That evening when he arrived home, he hugged my mother, then froze before her kitchen calendar.

"Why do you have that date circled?"

"I don't know. I just couldn't rest until I circled it. Why?"

"Because I circled the same date on my calendar at work."

They clung to each other, pausing to pray for their three sons half a world away and whatever the coming days might bring. The night prior to the circled date my mother dreamed about me. All night she dreamed I was walking, walking, running. She awoke with an uneasiness that lingered. Now she knew which of her sons was in jeopardy. Throughout the day and night on the circled calendar date she and my father prayed for me.

Eventually, a telegram came. I was safe, although captured by the Swiss. The date I was shot down was the circled date on their calendars. I believe their prayers for me on that date in 1944 gave me the direction to cross over.

≈

Hugh Asbury Neely was a bombardier with the 720th Squadron, 450th Bombardment Group flying missions out of Manduria, Italy. He was discharged from the air force in 1945 and returned to Spartanburg, South Carolina. He died September 11, 1991.

≈

*The ultimate measure of a man
is not where he stands in moments of
comfort and convenience,
but where he stands at times
of challenge and controversy.*

MARTIN LUTHER KING, JR.

WHO PACKED YOUR PARACHUTE?

CAPTAIN CHARLIE PLUMB
FORMER NAVY FIGHTER PILOT

Recently, I was sitting in a restaurant in Kansas City. A man about two tables away kept looking at me. I didn't recognize him. A few minutes into our meal he stood up and walked over to my table, looked down at me, pointed his finger in my face and said, "You're Captain Plumb."

I looked up and said, "Yes, sir, I'm Captain Plumb."

He said, "You flew jet fighters in Vietnam. You were on the aircraft carrier *Kitty Hawk*. You were shot down. You parachuted into enemy hands and spent six years as a prisoner of war."

"How in the world did you know all that?"

"Because I packed your parachute."

I was speechless. I staggered to my feet and held out a very grateful hand of thanks. This guy came up with just the proper words. He grabbed my hand, he pumped my arm and said, "I guess it worked."

"Yes, sir, indeed it did," I said, "and I must tell you I've said a lot of prayers of thanks for your nimble fingers, but I never thought I'd have the opportunity to express my gratitude in person."

"Were all the panels there?"

"I must shoot straight with you. Of the eighteen panels that were supposed to be in that parachute, I had fifteen good ones. Three were torn, but it wasn't your fault, it was mine. I jumped out of that jet fighter at a high rate of speed, close to the ground. That's what tore the panels in the chute. It wasn't the way you packed it.

"Let me ask you a question," I said. "Did you keep track of all the parachutes you pack?"

"No," he responded, "it's enough gratification for me just to know that I've served."

I didn't get much sleep that night. I kept thinking about that man. I kept wondering what he might have looked like in a navy uniform—a Dixie cup hat, a bib in the back of the shirt, and bell bottom trousers. I wondered how many times I might have passed him on board the *Kitty Hawk*. I wondered how many times I might have seen him and not even said "good morning," "how are you," or anything, because, you see, I was a fighter pilot and he was just a sailor.

How many hours did he spend on that long wooden table in the bowels of that ship weaving the shrouds and folding the silks of those chutes? I could have cared less—until one day my parachute came along and he packed it for me. So the philosophical question here is this: How's your parachute packing coming along? Who looks to you for strength in times of need? And perhaps, more importantly, who are the special people in your life who provide you the encouragement you need when the chips are down? Perhaps it's time right now to give those people a call and thank them for packing your chute.

Editor's note: Charles Plumb, a U.S. Naval Academy graduate, was a jet pilot in Vietnam. After seventy-five combat missions, his plane was destroyed by a surface-to-air missile. Plumb ejected and parachuted into enemy hands. He was captured and spent six years in a communist Vietnamese prison.

HURT HELPERS

★ ★ ★

CHUCK HOLTON
FORMER U.S. ARMY RANGER

F*amily.*

Lisa Bohn smiled as she entered the Protestant International Church in Islamabad, Pakistan. Even though it was about seven thousand miles from her home church in Virginia Beach, she was amazed at the spirit of family that pervaded this place. She missed her husband and two children dearly, but this place made her realize that there were few places in the world where she didn't have family. It was one of the many benefits of being a believer.

Lisa was actually Major Lisa Bohn, and she was in this church today because she had volunteered to be one of the first deployed from her army reserve civil affairs unit, the 354th Civil Affairs Brigade out of Riverdale, Maryland. She and her husband had prayed about the decision and came to believe that it was the right thing to do, even though it meant a one-year separation. It wasn't that she wanted to go, but that she felt called to go. So, at the end of January 2002, Major Bohn left for Islamabad to work with the army's civil affairs operation there. Their mission was to help the people of the country, working with the United Nations and other non-governmental organizations, to help people who had been victimized during the reign of the Taliban.

By March, she and a friend had found this Protestant International Church near the American embassy, and had begun attending services there. On this particular Sunday, March 17, about seventy people were in attendance. They began with prayer and singing. The mood was joyful as the sermon began. Lisa sat down and began making comments in her notebook.

Your security is not in your sincerity.

She had just penned these words when it happened. Lisa heard a commotion in the back of the room. She turned just in time to see a man in dark clothing throwing round objects into the assembled crowd with both hands. Someone yelled "Grenades! He's got grenades!"

Lisa dove for cover. There was a flash of light, an explosion. Pain. People were screaming as the room filled with haze. Chaos erupted like a volcano as people ran, or crawled for the exits. Lisa's ears were ringing.

After a few moments, the explosions had stopped. Lisa immediately began tending to the wounded, realizing that at least one of the terrorists had been killed by his own grenade. Her legs were bleeding from multiple shrapnel wounds.

But others had fared much worse. One person who had been in the pew in front of her was killed. Two people in the pew behind her also died. In all, there were five fatalities in the attack, and forty-five people were injured.

Two days later, Lisa was awarded the purple heart by General Tommy R. Franks, Commander in Chief, U.S. Central Command, before returning home. Major Bohn credits her instinctive reaction to the training, which taught her how to respond to incoming fire, training that probably saved her life. She also believes, however, that God must have more for her to accomplish here on earth. If she had perished in the church that day, though, at least she would have been among family. She doesn't fear death, claiming Matthew 10:28, the verse that she held onto during her deployment in Afghanistan. "Do not be afraid of those who kill the body but cannot kill the soul. Rather, be afraid of the One who can destroy both soul and body in hell."

Lisa Bohn isn't normally the type to get a tattoo, but today she has several—tattoos of the purple heart medal, covering the scars on her legs caused by the shrapnel. And she hasn't let the cowardly acts of brutal men stop her from continuing in her service to those who need it, as she continues to play a vital role in her civil affairs unit during Operation Iraqi Freedom. One thing has changed, though—the license plate on her mini-van. Today it reads TUFFMOM.

≈

*None who have always been
free can understand the terrible fascinating
power of the hope of freedom
to those who are not free.*

PEARL S. BUCK

CHRISTMAS IN KOREA

✮✮✮

Larry Ebsch

When North Korean troops stormed across the thirty-eighth parallel in June 1950 to attack the outmanned South Korean forces, they triggered the Korean War, a bitterly fought conflict that lasted more than three years. As a U.S. Army medic stationed there, I witnessed the tiny country battered by bombings, artillery fire, and ground fighting.

Some fifty-four thousand U.S. troops died in the fighting, and South Koreans lost their homes by the thousands. But the part of the war that seemed to hit me hardest was the Korean orphans, children who had lost their parents in the bloodshed or who had been separated from them in the desperate rush to safety.

My days were exhausting, a never-ending supply of wounded or sick GIs occupying almost all of my time. Duty was lonely and scary, but whenever we started feeling sorry for ourselves, we needed only to look at those parentless children with confused faces and little hope for the future. It strengthened our resolve to protect them and their country from an enemy that was determined to overtake their homeland, no matter the cost.

Winters in Korea were brutally cold, but as Christmas approached in 1952, we were warmed by the care packages from home that began to arrive. They weren't much—homebaked bread and cookies, candy, chewing gum, reading materials, a few personal items—anything that could survive a trip of a few thousand miles. But just being able to open a package from home and read the letter inside lifted our spirits immensely.

Determined not to let the holiday pass feeling sorry for ourselves, the guys in my small unit made a makeshift Christmas tree out of a winter coat. We decorated the conceptual tree with some of the treats from home, a few knitted hats and gloves, and even some old socks with holes in them. It looked pitiful, but at least it was something, we thought.

Christmas Day arrived, and after our somewhat half-hearted celebration, my thoughts turned to the children in the local orphanage. They had no family or gifts, and though I knew they were in good hands with the sisters who ran the orphanage, I kept thinking, *Everyone deserves a Christmas, no matter where they live.*

"Let's go visit those kids at the orphanage," I suggested to my buddies. Surely, we could scrounge up something to give them. They agreed, and the four of us rounded up some Spam and crackers from our supplies, and wrapped the cookies, candy, and gum we'd been sent from home in old newspapers we found around our hut. We jumped into one of our ambulances and drove to the orphanage—a converted school building somewhere near Chonju. We didn't really know what we were getting ourselves into and hadn't really thought much about it, beyond the fact that we just wanted some kids to be happy on Christmas.

We couldn't call ahead to tell the nuns we were coming, but we hoped they would approve of our surprise visit. Of course, they did. When we finally arrived at the orphanage, they took one look at us with our arms full of presents and began hugging us and crying. Pulling us along, they led us to a large room where boys and girls of various ages—from toddlers to kids about eight years old—were eating a meager meal.

When the children saw us, their faces lit up. Visitors! "GI! GI!" they squealed. They surrounded us, and as we handed out the crudely wrapped parcels, the room filled with their cries of excited delight. Then the nuns asked us to sit down so the children could give us something. The sisters had apparently taught the orphans a few simple Christmas carols, for they began singing with enthusiasm. We sat, spellbound, tears running down our faces as we listened to their sweet singing. Their voices carried us home, far away from the discomfort and hardship that surrounded all of us.

Then it was time to leave, and as we stood, the children crowded around us again, tugging on our pants, hugging our legs and crying, "Thank you, GI! Thank you, GI!" over and over. We were so overwhelmed that we choked back more tears. Gently, we untangled ourselves from the children and made our way to the door.

As we climbed back into the ambulance, I thought that by all accounts this holiday should have been miserable, offering nothing but loneliness, bitter cold, some ragtag gifts, a few carols. But as we bounced along the road back to our barracks on the cold, long drive, the night seemed warm and full of promise. It seemed like—Christmas.

DREAMS OF A FLYING FUTURE

VENNA BISHOP

You think when you are sixteen years old, you are going to want a car. These were my thoughts as I looked at my infant son, Brian. Little did I realize that instead of a car, he would be more interested in pulling -3 to +9Gs and soaring through the air at 1500 miles per hour in an F-16 fighter. Just how this nineteen-inch left-handed baby turned into a six-foot-two-inch man, able to curl himself inside a sophisticated state-of-the-art cockpit, and have the time of his life as commander of the United States Air Force Thunderbirds Flying Demonstration Team was beyond this mother's wildest dreams.

Brian always had his head in the clouds, so to speak. As a youngster he was fascinated with the wind. He would try to sneak his hand out of the car window, hoping Mom would not catch his antics. Running with pinwheels and flying kites fascinated him. In fact, his favorite high school graduation gift was a parafoil kite. Santa brought Brian his first jet at age five. It was a pedal variety. He spent hours pedaling and riding it up and down the driveway, which was a perfect make-believe runway. Perhaps these were the interests that led to his aeronautical engineering degree.

Goals are dreams with deadlines. Brian was only eight years old when he attended a graduation ceremony at the U.S. Air Force Academy. He idolized the cadets in their uniforms and all the pomp and circumstance that surrounded events at the Academy. Over the majestic Rocky Mountains of Colorado's Rampart Range emerged six red, white, and blue Thunderbird jets in delta formation performing a magnificent clover loop over the stadium. Brian's adrenaline piqued at the sound of the afterburners, as he watched these planes move in unison past small puffy clouds with effortless ease. He knew, from that moment on, he wanted to fly jets.

Attend any Thunderbird Air Show and you will easily spot the family members sporting red, white, and blue Thunderbird insignia clothing and hats. As I've watched some of the parents at shows, I've observed a sense of pride in their son's or daughter's selection to this elite team. I couldn't help but notice their faces tighten as they watch this young adult (the same one they told a dozen times to pick up their clothes) perform almost effortlessly the tasks required of them. Suddenly their eyes glisten with moisture. It is an awesome, indescribable feeling, shared by every parent who ever had a son or daughter as a member of the team.

As I visit with Thunderbird parents at air shows, I ask them about the kinds of toys or activities their children were involved with as youngsters. The stories have much in common; almost all pilots, for example, had childhood interests in some form of transportation. Flying was never far from their imaginations. Their child's creativity was unleashed on everything from paper planes to model building.

Almost thirty years later, I watched Brian stand before a giant American flag in his blue flight suit and accept the Thunderbirds squadron banner for the change of command ceremony. But in my mind, I was recalling a day long ago, when Brian was an eleven-year-old in a Boy Scouts uniform. He marched down the center aisle of the Air Force Academy Cadet Chapel, carrying the American flag for the Memorial Day services. It was the beginning of his dream to attend the academy.

Reality set in when I saw Brian living his dream. From the cockpit of an F-16 Thunderbird on the end of a real runway, before thousands of spectators, his voice booms over the loudspeaker: "Good afternoon. The Thunderbirds are proud to dedicate this performance to the men and women of Point Mugu Naval Air Station. Thunderbirds, release brakes, ready now! Burners now!"

Prayer of a Confederate Soldier

✦ ✦ ✦

I asked God for health, that I might do greater things;
    I was given infirmity, that I might do better things.
I asked for strength, that I might achieve;
    I was made weak, that I might learn to obey.
I asked for riches, that I might be happy;
    I was given poverty, that I might be wise.
I asked for power, that I might have the praise of men;
    I was given weakness, that I might feel the need of God.
I asked for all things, that I might enjoy life;
    I was given real life, that I might enjoy all things.
I got nothing I asked for, but everything I had hoped for;
    Almost despite myself, my unspoken prayers were answered.
    I am, among all men, most richly blessed.

A PRAYER FOUND IN THE POCKET OF A YOUNG, UNKNOWN CONFEDERATE SOLDIER
WHO MET HIS DEATH ON A CIVIL WAR BATTLEFIELD.

FOLLOWING
HIS PURPOSE

★★★

CHUCK HOLTON
FORMER U.S. ARMY RANGER

Some people find Mike a bit curious.

He's earned advanced degrees from Ivy League schools and, before he became a Christian, pursued a traditional corporate career, but has chosen not to pursue the wealth or prestige that could accompany those accomplishments.

Curious, because he enjoys helping soldiers, though he was never one himself.

Few people look and act less like a soldier, in fact. Mike is more likely to be taken for a good-natured scientist or slightly eccentric professor. But Mike is comfortable with his role in life. He lives simply, supporting himself on a teacher's meager salary.

But there is one thing about soldiers that Mike has come to understand—he knows they need to save a piece of themselves from an army culture that has led many a young man astray. He provides them a place to go, a home-away-from-home, where they can kick back and remember who they are, if only for a while. At Mike's they can forget about being Private Cook or Sergeant Williams, and just be Dave or Phil.

In a way, this is Mike's calling.

To serve the servicemen, Mike has mentored more than a dozen young infantrymen, who, fresh from basic training at Fort Benning, were away from home for the first time. It's become a ministry of sorts as he volunteers to pick these men up from the barracks and drive them to church or the movies or to get a haircut. His living room has played host to many movie and pizza nights, as well as Bible studies and deep spiritual conversations.

For more than a decade now, Mike has been a loyal friend to these soldiers, always available if help is needed. Because of the generosity he's displayed, Mike has collected nearly a platoon of fiercely devoted, lifelong friends.

I should know, because I was the first of those he ministered to back in 1987. If it weren't for his godly example and willingness to confront me when I was going wrong, my life would be drastically different today. And now my young brother-in-law, Cory, who is currently finishing Airborne school at Fort Benning, is the most recent army private that Mike has extended his friendship to. In the years between my time and Cory's, Mike has reached out to many others, and of those, he has even had the privilege to see some of them place their faith in Jesus and become recruits into God's army.

And some people find Mike a bit curious. Perhaps it's because he follows the pathway that God has set before him, regardless of what the world's expectations are. His life choices, to some, might seem unconventional, but people said the same about John the Baptist, and Jesus called him the greatest man that ever lived.

If that's the case, then maybe we should all aspire to be a little more *unconventional* ourselves.

COLD GUARD TOWER

★★★

TRAVIS PERRY

I was cold on the guard tower that night. It was cold every night, at least compared to the daytime temperature, which got up over one hundred.

I'd been activated as an army reservist in December 1990, and transferred from my unit in Denver to the 318th Evacuation Hospital, a reserve unit based in North Dakota. They'd flown me to Bismarck, where it was thirty-five degrees below zero. I'd helped load equipment there, in the biting cold.

Then they'd sent us to Fort McCoy, Wisconsin, where it was fifteen below zero. As we walked around in our arctic parkas, processing to be shipped overseas, someone joked in a Bill Murray voice, "What kind of training are we doing?" "Desert training, sir."

The 311th Evac Hospital went to the United Arab Emirates [the UAE], a small Gulf country that borders Saudi Arabia, in support of Operation Desert Storm. At first we'd felt we were baking in the Middle Eastern heat. But it didn't take long for our bodies to adjust to the daytime highs. So when the temperature fell into the forties at night—a sixty degree drop—we felt like we were freezing.

That's why my hands were numb as I held my M-16. In the distance, a car was driving in the desert, coming toward us.

Unlike Saudi Arabia, the UAE never expelled the Iraqi nationals living there. So while we were more than three hundred miles from Kuwait, we were considered prime targets for terrorists—threatcon Charlie.

I remember nervously calling in to the sergeant in charge of the guard, "Uh, there's someone out here." Because of the terrorism threat, we pulled guard duty with live rounds in the magazines of our ammo pouches, in positions that ringed the side of our camp facing the Arabian desert. But we rarely ever saw anyone out there. Especially not at night.

I don't remember what the sergeant told me, but I do remember the rules of engagement hadn't changed. We were not to fire unless fired upon.

The car drove toward us, close enough that it was illuminated by the spotlights we had shining out into the desert for perimeter security. Then the driver stopped. He sat there, for how long I don't know. My numb fingers loaded a magazine into the M-16.

And I watched him, hoping whoever it was would just turn around and go away. I'd become a medical specialist for a reason. I love my country and have always felt willing to die for it, but I didn't want to kill anyone.

Then the man stepped out of his car. It was a newer car, a European make, something that definitely didn't belong out where it was. He walked around to the trunk and opened it. Then he reached inside.

In my mind's eye I saw him picking up a rocket launcher and firing at us. I slipped a round into the chamber, my weapon still on safe. I knew at that moment, down to the very core of my being, that if the man came up from the trunk with a weapon aimed in our direction, I would kill him.

"Please, God, please," I prayed. Even in junior high, when I lost my temper far too easily and got into more than my fair share of fights, I always felt so guilty when I hurt someone, even if I was in the right. Even though it would've been right to shoot in order to protect our hospital, still, I didn't want to kill. "Please just let the man drive away."

Then the man pulled away from inside the trunk, not with a weapon, not even with a camera or a spare tire. As he looked up toward me, his hands rested on the open trunk, nothing in them at all.

Then he slammed the trunk shut and walked around to the front of the car. He got in the front seat and drove away. I never saw that car again.

I still wonder what he was doing out there, driving to a medical out-post in the middle of the night, opening his trunk. I suspect that whatever he was going to do, I wouldn't have liked it. But I'm thankful that I never found out what the man's intentions were and that I never fired a shot.

That night, as I watched the car disappear into the desert, my pound-ing heart warmed my body. As I thanked God for His mercy, the night didn't seem so cold.

*The only thing necessary
for the triumph of evil is
for good men to do nothing.*

EDMUND BURKE

FORMER ENEMIES

★ ★ ★

REVEREND PETER BALDWIN PANAGORE

Some years ago, while leading a church group on a tour of Pearl Harbor, I stood among the clergy and their spouses in the gleaming white-arched and covered memorial above the USS *Arizona*. One minister in our group, a man from Maine, had been there on December 7, 1941—the day the Japanese flew in to sink our Pacific naval fleet. He had not been aboard the *Arizona*, but his ship had also been hit. He described vividly the horrors of being aboard the flaming and sinking vessel as bullets flew and bombs roared. As I listened, out of the corner of my eye, I noticed a Japanese tourist entering the memorial.

It was the man's fine clothes—long tie, buttoned sports jacket, and shiny brown lace-up shoes—that initially attracted my attention. In Hawaii, professionals like lawyers, corporate executives, soldiers, and ministers seldom, if ever, wear ties or jackets. Even network television news anchors wear open-collared aloha shirts. This man, dressed as he was, stood out.

Two women walked with him. The older one I took to be his wife, the other perhaps an older daughter. Both wore conservative dresses and fancy shoes. The man appeared to be in his sixties, and while he may have spoken English, I only heard him speak Japanese. In his left hand, he carried, almost shyly, an ornate and obviously costly multiflowered wreath about eighteen inches across.

Our group's veteran continued to speak as we clustered around him. He described being caught below deck, feeling disoriented as the ship took on water where he stood, fire coming from above and the smoke stealing his breath. His buddy lay dead at his feet as the young sailor struggled in the darkness to escape, fear and adrenaline propelling him to the surface. Everyone in our group was so engrossed in his story that no one, except for me, noticed the Japanese tourist and his family who walked quite near us.

As I watched, the tourist stopped, turned to his wife and daughter and spoke to them. They stood quietly, almost solemnly. Then the man straightened his tie, first at the neck and then near the belt, and tugged at the hem of his jacket. As if in preparation, he squared his shoulders, took a deep breath and then exhaled. Alone, he somberly stepped forward toward the railing at the water's edge above the sunken warship.

The other tourists swirled around him. From what I could see and hear, they were apparently all Americans. They were talking, laughing, looking, asking questions; some were listening to our minister's story, but none seemed aware of the tourist who had captured my attention.

I don't believe the Japanese man understood the minister's words. As I listened to one man and watched the other, the Japanese tourist came to the rail, bowed at the waist and then stood erect. He began to speak; I heard his words but could not comprehend them. From his tone and the look on his face, however, I felt their meaning. His manner conveyed so many things at once—confession, sorrow, hurt, honor, dignity, remorse, and benediction.

When he had finished his quiet prayer, he gravely dropped the flowered wreath into the seawater—the same water the minister kept mentioning in his reminiscence—and watched as the wreath floated away on the tide. The man struggled to remain formal, to keep face, but his tears betrayed him. I guessed he must have been a soldier, a warrior of the air, whose own plane had showered the bombs and bullets that had torn through our soldiers, sinking their ships. It struck me that he had come on a pilgrimage of repentance, not to our government, but to the gravesite of those young men whose lives he had taken in the name of war.

Stepping backward one pace, the Japanese veteran then closed his eyes and bowed again, very deeply and very slowly from the waist. Then he stood tall, turned around, and rejoined his family. His deed done, they began to leave. All the while, our minister veteran continued his narrative. He and the group were oblivious to the poignant counterpoint occurring behind them.

But I was not the only American to witness the Japanese man's actions. As I watched his family leave, I noticed another American step away from the wall on which he had been leaning. He was dressed casually and wore a red windbreaker with the VFW emblem on it. He had a potbelly and thinning hair, and he held his hat in his hand. I assumed the man was a World War II veteran. *Perhaps he had served in the Pacific,* I thought, *and is himself on a pilgrimage.*

As the Japanese family walked by him, the American stepped directly into their path, blocking their way. I immediately tensed, fearing a confrontation. The startled Japanese tourist, who had been deep in thought, stopped short, surprise and sorrow mixed on his face. His family, eyes on the ground, stopped abruptly, then crowded closer around him.

But the American simply stood at attention, once again a strong, straight-backed soldier. Then he raised his right hand slowly and stiffly to his forehead, saluting his former enemy.

The American remained in salute until the Japanese, with dawning understanding, returned the gesture.

As the tourists milled by, the two men stood as if alone, joined by their shared pain, glories, honors, and memories, until the American, while remaining at attention, slowly lowered his arm and formally stepped backward one pace. The Japanese tourist, when his arms were both once again at his side, bowed formally to the man in front of him. To my surprise, the American returned the honor.

Neither said a word. Neither had to. Their solemn faces, wet with tears, communicated with each other in a universal language what never could have been said in words.

I watched as the two men, their reconciliation complete, went their separate ways, united in a way I had never imagined possible.

COMING HOME

***

DAVID REDDING
FROM *JESUS MAKES ME LAUGH*

I remember going home from the navy for the first time during World War II. Home was so far out in the country that when we went hunting we had to go toward town. We had moved there for my father's health when I was just thirteen. We raised cattle and sheep.

I started a little flock of Shropshire sheep, the kind that are completely covered by wool except for a black nose and the tips of black legs. My father assisted them when they had their twins at lambing time, and I could tell each one of the flock apart at a distance with no trouble. I had a beautiful ram. Next door was a poor man who had a beautiful dog and a small flock of sheep he wanted to improve with my ram. He asked me if he could borrow the ram; in return he would let me have the choice of the litter from his prize dog.

That is how I got Teddy, a big, black Scottish shepherd. Teddy was my dog, and he would do anything for me. He waited for me to come home from school. He slept beside me, and when I whistled he ran to me even if he were eating. At night no one could get within a half mile without Teddy's permission. During those long summers in the fields I would only see the family at night, but Teddy was with me all the time. And so when I went away to war, I didn't know how to leave him. How do you explain to someone who loves you that you are leaving him and will not be chasing woodchucks with him tomorrow like always?

So, coming home that first time from the navy was something I can scarcely describe. The last bus stop was fourteen miles from the farm. I got off there that night at about eleven o'clock and walked the rest of the way home. It was two or three in the morning before I was within a half mile of the house. It was pitch dark, but I knew every step of the way. Suddenly Teddy heard me and began his warning bark. Then I whistled only once. The barking stopped. There was a yelp of recognition, and I knew that a big black form was hurtling toward me in the darkness. Almost immediately he was there in my arms. To this day that is the best way I can explain what I mean by coming home.

What comes home to me now is the eloquence with which that unforgettable memory speaks to me of my God. If my dog, without any explanation, would love me and take me back after all that time, wouldn't my God?

FAITH ON THE
FRONT LINES

GREAT TRUTHS

Prayer for others is a generous act.
It sweeps away bitterness and heals old wounds.
Prayer leads to greater humility and a more grateful spirit.
It strengthens our commitment to things that last and things that matter.
It deepens our love for one another.
Prayer also deepens faith, reminding us of great truths:
Evil and suffering are only for a time; love and hope endures.

PRESIDENT GEORGE W. BUSH

BAPTISM IN THE SAND

⭐ ⭐ ⭐

Lynne M. Thompson

The world watched the peculiar ceremony on television. The man was Army Specialist James Kiehl, arms crossed and eyes closed, being immersed in a makeshift baptismal dug in the sand in the Kuwaiti desert. It looked like a watery graveside service, and in a way it was. The believer's baptism has always symbolized a kind of death—a death to self.

At age twelve, James left his California home and went to live with his father and stepmother in Texas. There in the Bible belt, his stepmother gave him a healthy dose of Christianity. Even though James was willing to acknowledge the existence of a Supreme Being, he was hesitant to embrace the gospel of Christ. His stepmother respected his need to wait and vowed to pray for his future conversion.

James grew up and eventually married Jill, a believer who made it her mission to gently share with him the love of Christ as his stepmother had done.

When James was twenty-one, he met a fellow soldier at Fort Bliss, Texas, who was serving as an assistant chaplain. James accepted Christ, but decided to wait to be baptized. For some reason, he sensed that it just wasn't time.

As talk of the war on Iraq loomed, James and his wife decided to postpone having a family. James didn't want to be deployed and chance missing the birth of their first baby. But God had other plans. Despite their precautions, Jill became pregnant with a son, and James was called to serve overseas.

Then, while stationed in Kuwait, hours from joining the battle in Iraq, James asked to be baptized. It was time. It wasn't because he thought he wouldn't go to heaven if he never completed the ritual, but because he felt that some of his fellow soldiers needed to see it. A hole was dug, plastic laid, and precious drinking water donated. Cameramen captured the occasion; a witness to the world that what really matters is not the battle for a nation or an ideal, but for the souls of men.

A few days later, the convoy that James was riding in took a wrong turn and entered enemy territory, where they were ambushed. His body was found days later at the hospital where Private Jessica Lynch was rescued, along with the bodies of some of the others on the ill-fated mission.

Specialist James Kiehl's family takes comfort in their son's public demonstration of his faith. And the setting was especially timely and poignant. Their hope is that his example will encourage other soldiers to find hope in God.

SIXTY DAYS IN
THE WILDERNESS

Chuck Holton
Former U.S. Army Ranger

Mike Sonnenschein is a driven man.
His résumé reads like that of a real-life action figure:

> black belt in tae kwon do
> former motocross racer
> decorated combat veteran
> airborne ranger
> sport parachutist

Live hard, work hard, and play harder. Mike seems to have acquired this motto early in life. As early as junior high school, Sonny, as his friends called him, attacked every challenge as if his life depended on it. He was a classic overachiever and developed an insatiable appetite for adventure.

Though he grew up in a loving home, it was a completely secular one. Without a spiritual underpinning, Mike saw no reason not to experiment with alcohol, and even drugs, as early as junior high. By senior high, partying had become almost a way of life.

But nothing ever did it for him, and he wasn't even sure what "it" was. What he did know was that every achievement left him empty and every adventure was a letdown.

After graduation, Mike joined the army and naturally gravitated to the best of the best—the rangers. He found there a group of men much like himself—men whose motto included the phrase "one hundred percent and then some." He excelled in the unit and even won the vaunted Best Ranger competition in 1989, making him something of a legend in the ranger community. He continued to chase accomplishments, and they continued to let him down.

In 1990, his unit deployed to Saudi Arabia. Mike wasn't exactly happy about it, but when the army says go, you go. As they were preparing to ship out, a chaplain showed up and began handing out New Testaments to the troops. Mike's friend, a fellow staff sergeant named Bill, turned to him and said, "Hey, Sonny, let's go get a Bible. There won't be anything else to read over there." Sonny knew he was right. The normal vices that usually occupied his time would be prohibited in the Middle East, so he figured he'd need whatever diversion he could get.

When they reached the chaplain, Bill said, "Hey, sir, you wouldn't happen to have any copies of the complete Bible, would you?"

The chaplain stopped and looked at the two soldiers, as if trying to gauge if they were serious. Then he said, "I'll be right back."

He returned in a few moments, carrying two of his personal Bibles, which he gave to Mike and his buddy. "Take good care of them," he said. Mike put the book in his rucksack and promptly forgot about it.

A short time later, Mike and Bill found themselves in a four-man Bedouin tent in the middle of the Saudi desert. As the days wore on and their unit spent less and less time training, Mike spent more and more time sitting on his bunk, baking in the heat and thinking about his life. One question kept coming to the surface of his thoughts.

What's it all about?

The Bible was still in his rucksack, untouched. One day he saw Bill reading his copy, and it got Mike thinking of the old movie, *The Ten Commandments,* that he had watched on television as a kid. The story had always fascinated him, perhaps because his father's family came from a Jewish heritage.

"Hey, Bill," Mike said. "Where would I find the story of the Ten Commandments in there?"

Bill thought for a moment. "Exodus, I think."

Mike looked up Exodus in the table of contents and turned to that page. What he read blew him away. He had always thought of the Bible as an arcane collection of *begats,* but now he realized that it had some intriguing stories in it. The Old Testament stories came alive, perhaps because he was living in a primitive tent in the very land where the stories had taken place, or maybe because he was finally ready to hear the stories. Whatever the reason, he was enthralled.

He moved on to the New Testament. As he read, he began to evaluate his lifestyle. By the time he got to the book of Romans, he knew that he needed a change, and that it was time.

The more he read, the more he found himself believing. No one had ever taught him the "right" things to pray, but he began to talk to God anyway, awkwardly at first.

And that's when it happened. He could feel a change inside. Something began to fill that void that he had tried so desperately to fill with adventure, liquor, achievement, and fun. It was a wonderful feeling. He drank in the books of the Bible like a man who has just discovered water in the desert. And indeed, he had.

After two months in Saudi Arabia, Mike finally got sent home. When he got back to Fort Benning, the first thing he did was go out to a club with some of his army buddies out of sheer habit. But something was wrong. He now felt out of place in a setting that had once felt like home. He knew that he no longer belonged there.

Over the next several months, Mike got involved with a church and pursued his newfound faith with the same intensity that had made him successful in everything else. He now realized what idols those accomplishments had been to him and so he began to get rid of the trappings of his success. He threw away plaques and trophies, burned his black belt, and gave away the custom-engraved 9-mm pistol he had won during the Best Ranger competition. His friends thought he had completely lost it. Overnight he became "Sonny, the Jesus freak" to his former friends.

But he no longer needed their approval. He had found what he had been looking for and was saved from a meaningless life.

THE HELMET AND
THE SWORD

Marilyn K. McAuley and
Lance Corporal Daniel Eugene Coleman
United States Marine Corps

Dan's knee bounced nervously as we waited to hear final instructions to the marines and their families. He loved being a marine. No man in that room could be any more proud than our nineteen-year-old grandson. But the future was unknown, and though he was well prepared for it, he was anxious—and so was I. He had never seen anyone die before. I knew seeing blood bothered him and that he wondered about such things as being a POW or an MIA—or if he would even return home again. I knew our thoughts commingled, we just couldn't verbalize them. If we didn't say them out loud, perhaps they wouldn't happen. He was now a marine, after all, and such concerns he kept to himself. Only a bouncing knee gave action to his innermost feelings.

Dan and I discovered that writing letters to each other is comforting and encouraging. We talk about the Lord and share verses from the Bible that mean something special to us. Our letters flew back and forth while he attended military high school and then more so when he went to boot camp. Now it is the end of January 2003. War with Iraq is on the threshold, and he is just days away from leaving with his platoon to serve in Operation Iraqi Freedom.

I study his young, chiseled face, his cap squared on his head with the bill over his eyes, not down the back of his neck, as was his habit. He loves wearing his ballcaps. Now he's trading them in for a helmet that I pray will save his life, if necessary. He senses me watching him. We smile. I hand him an envelope. "Here is your first letter of this campaign." The knee stops bouncing long enough to slip it into the pocket on his cami's pant leg. Later, when very much alone, he would read:

January 27, 2003
Dearest Grandson,

G-pa and I are so proud of you. Thank you for fighting for our freedom. God is with you at all times. Rest in Him... Your great-grandpa was a loyal sailor who fought for our nation's freedom during World War II. The Bible he carried in his pocket then is now yours. Carry it with dignity and let the words comfort and encourage you just as they did for him so many decades ago.

A favorite chapter of mine in the Bible is Philippians 4. I want to share verses 6–7 with you now. "Do not be anxious about anything, but in everything, by prayer and petition, with thanksgiving, present your requests to God. And the peace of God, which transcends all understanding, will guard your hearts and your minds in Christ Jesus."

Dan, this peace of God is beyond our ability to comprehend but it guards us as believers. The term *guard* translates a military term, which means, "to protect or garrison by guarding." Like soldiers assigned to watch over a certain area, God's peace garrisons our hearts and minds.

All my love and prayers,
G-ma

February 22, 2003
Dear Grandma and Grandpa,

You know, I thought I would be scared the moment I got off the plane, but I wasn't. I feel the Lord's presence. I wrote in my helmet these two passages from the Bible and they have helped.

Psalm 31:3: Thou art my rock and my fortress; therefore for thy name's sake lead me, and guide me.

I definitely feel that He is leading me.

Psalm 27:1: The Lord is my light and my salvation; whom shall I fear? The Lord is the strength of my life; of whom shall I be afraid?

I have felt no fear since being here. Every time I go out on my patrols I feel the Lord by my side watching my every move.

I love you and I thank you for your prayers. I am reading God's Word almost every day.

Love, your grandson,

Daniel Eugene Coleman

SEMPER FIDELIS! from Iraq!

Always faithful—to God and country.

As I read his letter I thought about our spiritual armor in Ephesians 6:17. Dan not only has a helmet to protect his head, but also the spiritual helmet of salvation. Now he's using the sword of the Spirit, the Word of God, to cover his head. Knowing that Scripture both fills his heart and covers his head gives me peace as I pray for him in the night watches.

Come home, Dan—come home.

LESSON FROM DESERT STORM

DR. DANNY SMITH
AS TOLD TO
KAYLEEN REUSSER

A succession of deafening explosions ripped through the night, awakening me from a fitful sleep. Immediately, I put on my gas mask and bolted from the cot to join other personnel at the barracks windows.

Black smoke and flying debris obliterated our view of the war-torn Kuwaiti desert. The cacophony of noise sounded different from the other times when we had been fired at by one of Saddam Hussein's low-flying Soviet Scud missiles. Later we learned that a seventeen-foot Allied rocket, the Patriot, had streaked through the sky, breaking the sound barrier and blowing away an incoming Scud in a fiery collision.

It was history's first wartime intercept of a ballistic missile. A television crew on the roof of a nearby building caught the event on film so millions of American viewers could watch it.

I was platoon commander of the Army National Guard medical unit stationed out of Iowa City, Iowa. This unit had been deployed to Kuwait in January 1991 as part of a massive military buildup by the United States to combat Saddam Hussein's invasion of Kuwait. Our mission was to perform advance trauma life support, stabilize the wounded, and send them back to the MASH unit or field hospital in the rear.

We hadn't been there long when medical intelligence told us that due to an increase in air strikes, we should expect five hundred to one thousand casualties a day.

The news, heat, stress of waiting, and our proximity to danger created a palpable tension within camp. It was my duty to maintain order. Thus far, I had done so, but I wondered how long it would last.

As a Christian, I often sought help from the Scriptures. Psalm 91, in particular, gave me strength and courage. "For it is he who delivers you...from the deadly pestilence" (v. 3) could refer to biological and chemical warfare. Verse 5 says, "You will not be afraid of the terror by night." I took that to mean the Scud missile attacks.

The words, written thousands of years ago, seemed to fit our twentieth-century situation amazingly well and never failed to give me peace that God was in control.

I had always believed everyone dealt with God in his or her own way and never forced my faith on anyone. But as the days passed and tension grew, I questioned my motives. Was I keeping silent about my faith out of concern for others or because I was afraid of what others would think? That night I was ashamed to realize it was the latter and I prayed for wisdom.

The next day, Bible in hand, I ordered the entire platoon to assemble in the mess hall. "No one knows when this thing will end or if any of us will walk away from it. I've been scared and I think most of you have been too. But I believe Someone greater than Saddam is watching over us right now; Someone who cares what happens to us. God, our Creator, loves us and is able to protect us." Then I read the sixteen verses of Psalm 91.

They were so familiar I could have read them with my eyes closed. That day, however, they took on new meaning as my voice rang out with conviction. "He who dwells in the shelter of the Most High will abide in the shadow of the Almighty...."

Afterward, I said a short prayer, then dismissed the platoon. Several people thanked me for reading the Scriptures. I noticed soldiers reading the New Testaments issued to them during the next few days.

However, it wasn't until two days later, when 160 of us were sent up to the front line to support the 3rd Artillery Division from 7th Corps out of Europe, that I saw how powerful God's Word could be. Dug in bunkers, two kilometers behind the Iraqi-Saudi border, we waited for the 100-hour Ground War to start.

When it did start on February 24, the number of casualties in our unit increased, but they were mostly minor shrapnel injuries. We never did have the hundreds of battle-related casualties that medical intelligence had predicted.

When the Allied forces called a truce with Saddam, we praised God that our entire unit escaped with little injury. A few weeks later, our platoon returned safely to the States.

After a warm reception from my family and a period of rest, I resumed my private practice. Everything appears to be the same in my life as it was before the Gulf War.

But it's not.

Now I pray with patients who are having a tough time. I share with colleagues the things God is doing in my life. When one doctor friend left the States to begin missionary work in Africa, I read Psalm 91 at his going-away party.

The Gulf War was a difficult time of separation for my family and me, but if given the opportunity to serve my country overseas again, I would. I believe in the ideals this country stands for and will do everything I can to see that they are carried out in other nations.

THE HAND OF GOD

★ ★ ★

LeRoy "Pete" Petersohn
as told to Tricia Goyer

There are many memories of war that last a lifetime. Memories of buddies lost right before one's eyes, of prisoners, of battle. Sometimes these memories meet me at the strangest times, but there's one memory above all that has changed me forever.

Bastogne and the Battle of the Bulge can be considered no picnic. I was wounded there, and I remember sixty years ago as if it were yesterday. Our unit had been corralled in a low area. I was a medic, and this is where we'd based our headquarters.

As a medic, you go where you're needed. One day we received a radio message that they were desperate for medics in the next town. The infantry had taken severe punishment and they'd lost two medical men.

My medical officer approached me. "Come on, Pete, we've got to move out."

I'd been over talking to a couple radio operators, my good buddies. I said good-bye to my friends. Then I jumped in to drive the jeep, with Major Harold G. Stacy beside me, and we headed off. But to get to the next town we had to cross a high point, a very high point. We didn't know it at that time, but the Germans had that area pegged with their big 88-mm guns.

As we hit the top of that hill, a gun shell went over us. It landed about fifty feet away—at the most. The next one landed right in front of us. We knew then we had to abandon ship. The major jumped out one side, and I dove out the other. On my side of the road I spotted the slightest gully, and into it I jumped.

I knew I had little protection and figured I was a goner since the Germans were firing from my side. Then something amazing happened. As I lay there, I felt someone pushing on my back, pushing me deeper into the ground and telling me to get down.

Rounds three, four, and five landed on the jeep. There was nothing left. But as I lay in that ditch, I had a sensation of protection, one I'll never forget. When it was over, blood dripped from my nose and ears. The major was okay, but I had concussion problems from the shells that shook the ground. It took five days of rest before I could resume my duties. And even though I looked fine on the outside, something had changed within.

I'd been a Christian since I was a small child, but I had an even greater faith after feeling the protection of the Lord pressing upon me. I'm still a strong Christian today because of that experience. Many people can deny the fact that God exists, but not me. I've felt His hand…and heard His whisper in the midst of war.

~

PRAYER FROM KUWAIT

We covet your prayers for wisdom as future possibilities
place a burden on leaders to be effective while
simultaneously caring for their soldiers' safety.
I therefore ask that you pray that my judgment will be
sound and that my decisions will be precise.
For those prayers, I thank you.

LTC, ERIC WESLEY
ADAPTED AND USED BY PERMISSION OF *COMMAND* MAGAZINE, PUBLISHED BY
OFFICER'S CHRISTIAN FELLOWSHIP, ENGLEWOOD, COLORADO.

GOD IS MY AUTOPILOT

CHUCK HOLTON
FORMER U.S. ARMY RANGER

Will this night ever end?

Coast Guard Lieutenant Ted LeFeuvre groaned as the alert siren went off for the third time. He had just been ready to climb into bed, again, when it sounded. He dropped the sheets he'd been arranging on the bed in the duty room at the Coast Guard Air Station in New Orleans, Louisiana, and headed for the tarmac to fire up the orange and white HH-65 Dolphin helicopter. Again. He felt like someone was pulling a cruel joke on him.

I guess I'll get plenty of sleep when I'm dead.

He was soon joined by the rest of the aircrew, his copilot, a flight mechanic to run the winch, and a medic, or "health services technician" as they were called in the Coast Guard. All of them were clearly exhausted, but none of them complained a bit about having to go back up. He was proud to lead such selfless people.

Their first rescue that night had taken place around sundown. A small boat had gotten stuck in one of the many swamps that occur along the Mississippi delta. They had actually towed the boat to safety with a line lowered from the state-of-the-art helicopter. It was a good thing the Coast Guard didn't bill for towing—the fuel bill alone would have been many times the cost of the boat. But the rescuers didn't see it that way. They were just doing their job, and the relieved waves and smiles of the boaters below was all the payment they needed.

The second launch that night had been a reported emergency flare off shore. The crew had gone up and searched the area for more than an hour, and finding nothing, had returned to base.

As they lifted off the tarmac for the third time, it was already past 2 A.M., and Lieutenant LeFeuvre knew this mission was going to be a long flight. There were reportedly two fishermen, a disabled veteran and a diabetic, who had failed to return from their day of fishing off of the Chandeleur Islands, more than one hundred miles off shore from the Coast Guard station. It would take them at least a half an hour to get to the search area, and another half hour to get back. Ted breathed a silent prayer, as he always did on rescue missions, as he turned southeast into a moonless, overcast sky over the Gulf of Mexico. This time he was praying that God would guide them to the lost fishermen quickly.

The Dolphin came equipped with something called a "fully coupled flight director," which was basically a computer that could fly the craft in a programmed search grid so that the pilot was free to assist in the search. This was 1986, before the use of night vision equipment had become widespread. Looking for a small boat in the open ocean on a moonless night was kind of like trying to find a dropped contact at the beach, in the dark. The crew needed all the help they could get.

One thing Ted could see was his instruments. As the chopper thundered toward the search area, he began a routine scan of his gauges. *Altimeter, attitude, instruments, clock.* He'd done the check so often that it had become second nature. There was a rhythm to it, like breathing, as he scanned the backlit panel several times a minute.

Altimeter, attitude, instruments, clock.

Once they reached the vicinity where the fishermen had last been seen, LeFeuvre programmed the search grid into the flight director, and they began flying a rectangular grid, six miles long, half mile wide. The helicopter executed this with rigorous precision, as the crew's eyes turned outward to scan the dark water below.

Altimeter, attitude, instruments, clock.

After about thirty-five minutes, Ted noted that their fuel level was nearing the point at which they'd have to turn back. He was dog tired, but knew they had to keep looking.

Altimeter, attitude, instruments, clock.

Wait a minute! Something was wrong. He suddenly realized that more than twenty minutes had passed since he'd done his last check!

Horror hit him like a bucket of cold mud. *Did I fall asleep?*

He sat up quickly and looked at his copilot. The man was slumped forward, sound asleep. Behind them, the flight mechanic lay sprawled out on the floor of the aircraft, head lolling to one side. The medic looked like a wilted flower, drooped over her seat's restraining harness. No one aboard had been coherent for nearly a half hour.

Ted hit the intercom switch and started talking. "They've got to be out there somewhere." The other crew members' heads jerked upward in unison.

At that very moment, a signal flare went up directly in front of the helicopter.

Everything went into fast forward at that point. LeFeuvre flared the chopper hard to slow it down and swung around in a tight circle. It only took a moment to determine that the flare had, in fact, come from the lost fishermen, who were waving frantically from their small, open boat below. The crew quickly jumped to their tasks, and once the aircraft had stabilized in a hover, they were able to guide the medic down to them on a cable. Then they lowered a rescue basket to haul the men aboard.

Once the boaters were safely inside the aircraft and it had turned back toward base, Ted relaxed a little, smiled, and shook his head at what had just happened. He mouthed a quick prayer of thanks.

No one will ever convince Ted LeFeuvre that it was the computerized autopilot that flew them, by chance, to the exact place in that great big ocean where they needed to be, and then woke him up so they wouldn't miss the stranded fishermen below.

EVERY MAN
A WARRIOR

DAVE MEURER

Night had fallen by the time I drove up to the barricaded entrance of Edwards Air Force base. As one of the heavily armed airmen approached my vehicle, he glanced down at the recently expired air force identification sticker affixed to my bumper. His eyes widened for a moment as he counted the stripes, and he stood a bit more erect as he approached my window.

"Sir, are you a retired master sergeant?" he asked with a touch of awe in his voice.

For those of you who are not familiar with the military, I need to explain that anyone who achieves the rank of master sergeant is a rare breed and garners considerable respect among the brotherhood of soldiers.

I would have spent a few minutes chatting modestly about my many dangerous experiences were it not for the fact the most daring feat I had performed in the past decade was replacing an electrical outlet in the kitchen.

"Sorry," I replied. "I bought the car used, and a previous owner was in the air force. I tried, but it is a plastic bumper and the sticker is really fused on."

"Maybe we can scrape it off." He pulled out a pocket knife and scratched it across the bumper, to no avail.

"See what I mean?"

"Yeah. But maybe you can cover it up with something."

He was kindly diplomatic, but I was already translating his comment into, "It wouldn't really be right if someone mistook you for a professional soldier when the most aggressive thing you do on any given day is flail your barbecue mitt at the bees when you are cooking burgers."

"Good idea," I replied. "Thanks."

I filled out all the visitor information forms and drove to the home of my brother-in-law, who is a real air force sergeant who flies around in real air force planes and goes on real missions and stands in the open doorway of a gargantuan C-130 and gets combat pay for entering hostile airspace.

I felt miserably safe as the guard waved me past the barricades.

I've never been shot at. I've never thrown a grenade, even in practice. While I've been yelled at a few times, it was never by someone in uniform unless you count the Little League coach.

I think that, deep down, all guys want to be warriors. We want to be engaged in an epic battle where the stakes are high and where we matter. Where we rush the hill that must be taken. Where we can be heroes.

We can.

God has called us to be warriors, even if we never pick up a gun. That stuff the apostle Paul wrote about putting on the "full armor of God, so that you may be able to stand your ground" (Ephesians 6:13) was not a poetic flourish.

There really is a battle raging, and we really are in the thick of it.

When I confronted a friend who was about to ruin his marriage, I was in the battle. When I presented the claims of Christ to a group of teenagers late at night on a city street, I was wielding the sword of the Spirit in occupied territory. When I resist the powerful pull of sin, though sorely tempted to give in, I am repelling the enemy. When I simply cut a check to a missionary, I am resupplying the troops.

I am a soldier, and so are you. And we are in the greatest battle of the biggest war imaginable. And you matter.

GOD'S ARMY MEDAL

★ ★ ★

BILL GOTHARD

An important, classified mission in the Middle East was assigned to a task force of the 101st Airborne Division. Its commander gave orders to his brigade to carry out the mission on three different occasions, but all three times bad weather forced them to abort the effort. The next day, at their brigade update briefing, the commanding colonel summoned Chaplain Mike Shellman to report to the front of the room.

The colonel explained his frustration with the failed missions and stated, "Chaplain, I give up. There is nothing I can do. I want you to pray to God for good weather, so we can carry out this important mission. Give us a weather prayer, right now."

Chaplain Shellman cried out to the Lord on behalf of their task force and reminded God of His response to Elijah's cry for the weather and how He could do the same today.

The Colonel thanked him. "Let's see if God answers the chaplain's prayer."

On the following day, the air force weather reports were not encouraging for the base or the mission location, but the colonel ordered preparations to begin. Suddenly, God cleared up the weather in both locations. The mission was successfully carried out with no casualties.

The next evening, at the brigade update briefing, the colonel again asked the chaplain to report to the front of the room. "Chaplain, God answered your weather prayer, our mission went forth, and I am awarding you an Army Commendation Medal for your prayer and work." Then he read the following: "The Department of the Army has awarded the Army Commendation Medal to Chaplain Michael T. Shellman, Task Force Brigade Chaplain, for outstanding support to Task Force Rakkasan, for successfully petitioning the Lord God of Elijah to provide sufficient weather to enable Task Force Rakkasan to accomplish their mission." The colonel then pinned the medal on the chaplain's dusty uniform and asked him to address the commanders.

Chaplain Shellman told the group of God's power to change the weather and also to change lives through salvation. Then he prayed and thanked the Lord for answering their prayers.

～

We do well to apply the scriptural admonition that we should not be conformed to this world, but rather be transformed by the renewing of our minds. If we discover a "values gap," our strongest instinct should not be to conform to the lowest standard of behavior that goes unpunished elsewhere. Instead, we should seek the more earnestly to be worthy of the standards that others have neglected

ADMIRAL JAMES M. LOY
COAST GUARD CIVIL RIGHTS CONFERENCE

Excerpt from a Captain's Journal

★★★

It would be easy to set this time of my life aside and put everything on hold and lay my spiritual walk up on the shelf. I am away from my world, away from familiar surroundings. It would be easy to question how God could make good out of a family drawn apart—two young children missing their father, and a wife longing to be with her husband. Yet through the fog and mist of discouraging thoughts, the beams of God's radiance shine brilliantly through and scatter them away. Instead, I have chosen to mount up on wings like an eagle and soar with endurance while I wait upon the Lord.

My duration here is uncertain, and only time will tell of the future unknowns. But one thing I know to be abundantly clear—I have been brought here for an important mission (what an appropriate word that is). Yes, the air force has its goals and objectives, but even greater still, the Lord has brought me here for His own!

JASON LAY, UNITED STATES AIR FORCE
SERVING IN OPERATION IRAQI FREEDOM

PARACHUTE JUMP

★★★

STEVE WATKINS
PETTY OFFICER SECOND CLASS, SEAL TEAM FIVE

Tragedy struck, and I didn't have any idea what God was up to. On the day it happened, all I could do was catch my breath. It was a perfect Southern California day with crystal blue skies, little humidity, and a slight on-shore breeze. My Navy SEAL platoon had just returned from a seven-month deployment to Operation Desert Storm. We had been very successful accomplishing the most widely publicized SEAL operation in the Gulf—a diversion of Iraqi troops on Mina Saud beach in occupied Kuwait. But being back in California felt like the safest place on earth after numerous missions behind enemy lines.

I guess that's what made this day seem so incredibly surreal. After working in two platoons and even participating in combat, I was now assigned to SEAL Team Five's training department. I was the jumpmaster, and it was my responsibility to brief and prepare the men who were to parachute that day. The group I was briefing was new—just out of SEAL boot camp—but it was just a standard parachute drop.

Not once, but twice, I encouraged the men to watch out for other jumpers in order to avoid a midair collision, a common mistake of new jumpers. But they were raring to go and their adrenaline levels sent the message that they could fly without the need of an airplane. I told them to have a good jump and that I would see them later in the afternoon. While they went to the airfield where another jumpmaster would wave them out of the plane, I stayed behind.

I was sitting at my desk when the call came in from the drop zone. An accident had occurred on the jump. Two jumpers were injured, and one seriously. This couldn't be the same drop—not the guys I had briefed. But I knew there were no other jumpers scheduled that day. After hundreds of jumps, how could this happen to the guys just out of boot camp?

The Officer in Charge [OIC] of the training department came and told me what he knew. One jumper was doing pretty well with a badly sprained foot. The other jumper, however, was probably paralyzed from the waist down. The two parachutists had collided in midair when one jumper lost his awareness of the other jumpers. The resulting collision caused their parachutes to malfunction.

I went to the Naval Medical Center in San Diego the next day. At the hospital I met this young man's family. They were sobbing and his father had many questions. "Why my son? Why so young? What a waste!"

I was at a loss as to what to say. I was a Christian by that time and I brought a Bible with me to the hospital to give to the young man.

The father asked me if I thought God heard his prayers. I told him I knew that God not only hears our prayers, but is powerful to answer them as well.

A few days after the accident some interesting events transpired. Because the man who was paralyzed had been in a sixteen-man SEAL platoon that was nearing its six-month deployment date, a person was needed to fill the vacancy. The platoon needed someone with experience and one who could deploy in a couple of weeks.

In the platoon was a man who was, and still is, a hero to me. Mike had been a SEAL in Vietnam and was highly decorated for his many incredible SEAL missions. He had been one of my instructors when I was in boot camp. All the guys talked about Mike and how much he had accomplished. I was honored just to be his friend.

Mike was the chief of the platoon with the paralyzed jumper, and he asked me to fill the vacant position in the platoon. I was thrilled. I could hardly believe that I now had the opportunity to work with Mike. I accepted and we deployed for the Philippines a few weeks later.

I was the only Christian in the platoon. The other SEALs often poked fun at my being a follower of Christ. But they respected the fact that I was a good operator and they knew that I was willing to die for them.

One day while eating lunch with Mike, I began to share my faith with him. He was interested and began asking questions. Mike purchased a Bible at the base exchange and began reading the New Testament. Within two weeks, Mike had embraced Jesus Christ as his Lord and Savior. If that was not enough, within a month another platoon member, my roommate, Eric, also embraced Jesus Christ after many evening discussions and cups of coffee.

Only the wisdom and grace of God could have planned such a beautiful outcome of that tragic sunny California day. Now two of my closest SEAL friends are also my brothers in Christ. Mike is growing in the Lord and still calls to ask questions about the faith and the Bible. To this day, I am filled with wonder and awe at the plan of God and at how He uses *us* as part of that eternal plan.

Some things will never make sense in this life. Why the young SEAL with so much promise ahead of him was paralyzed will forever be a mystery. But I trust that God can answer our hard questions one day. Seeing how God used one man's tragedy to save Mike and Eric gives me hope that He can and will work all things together for good for those who truly love Him.

CHOICES

★ ★ ★

CHUCK DEAN, 173RD AIRBORNE BRIGADE

hoices. In Vietnam we had to make quite a few of them. Some were good and others were not so good.

I remember my third in-country parachute jump. We loaded up at Bien Hoa airbase on a Caribou, the funny looking aircraft that could land on fifty yards of landing strip, and headed out somewhere between the Iron Triangle and War Zone D in III Corp.

This was a routine training jump, and supposedly there were no hostile elements in the area. (However, I don't remember any area in Vietnam where there were *no* hostile elements.) It was a beautiful day; with ground temperatures at over one hundred degrees, the ride at two thousand feet was the closest thing to an air conditioner that any of us had felt in months. As cool as it was, we could have stayed up there all day, but it wasn't long before we were getting jump commands and were hooked up and waiting for the jumpmaster to send us back into the blistering countryside below.

I'd never jumped a Caribou before. C-119s, C-124s, C-130s, and UH 1D Huey choppers, yes—but never a plane like this. It was like stepping off your back porch. No prop blast, no hawk screaming at you. Just a walk in the park, so to speak. It was great.

After I exited the aircraft and my chute had opened, I checked everything out. I had a full canopy of air and no lines were tangled. Then I looked down and saw puffs of smoke and what seemed to be explosions going off. *Hey! This is supposed to be a training jump! Didn't anyone secure this DZ for us?*

Later on I found out that we had been dropped into an old French minefield that was laid during the French-Indochina War. We had no idea it was there. By mistake, we had been dropped into an uncharted area. However, from 1500 feet above I could not tell what the others were running into down below—I thought we had been dropped into a hot drop zone and were being attacked by communist forces.

Immediately I began to slip away from the area where all the commotion was taking place below. I began to drift toward a small lake to the left of me. Assessing my landing attitude, I was faced with one of those choices that I never expected to have to make as a paratrooper. I remembered in jump school when they told us all about water landings, and I began to rehearse it in my mind: *Hit your quick release and hang in the harness until about twenty feet off the water and then drop out of the chute into the water.* Nothing to it, right? Well, I suddenly had a question: What happens when you can't tell how deep the water is? Do you ride the 'chute in, hoping that it is shallow enough to do a good parachute landing fall? Or do I do what we were trained to do—fall free into the water? I knew that if I did, and the water was only ankle deep, I was at risk of breaking a leg or worse. On the other hand, if I rode it in and the water was over my head, getting safely out of the water without drowning was a problem, too.

I chose to stay in the chute and take my chances, and my premonition paid off. The choice was good. I landed in about six inches of muddy water and lived to fight another day.

Reflecting back on that incident and others while I was in Vietnam, I see the fingerprint of God all over them. I do know there were times, when under fire, that I would hug the ground and pray for God to save me. However, wanting to maintain an invincible attitude, I would brush myself off after the smoke cleared and merely think, *Well, I made it through another one.* Not once did I credit God for protecting me from the enemy's hands and even my own mistakes.

Being in control of situations became a way of life for me in Vietnam. Control meant life; control meant I had a choice in the matter, and no control meant death. It is interesting to look back and see that when I didn't have any choices and was at the mercy of my circumstances—was the next mortar round going to land in my back pocket or did the next sniper's bullet have my name on it? Only then did I cry out for something supernatural to happen. I remember asking God to save me, and I've often wondered since, *Did I believe in God then? Was I a believer?*

Over the years my life became ravaged by posttraumatic stress. The war raged on every day through the memories of my experiences in Vietnam. It was shortly after my forty-second birthday that my life was so far down all I could do was look up.

I made a life-changing phone call to another paratrooper from another war. My friend Bill had fought in Korea and I confided in him that I had come to the end of the trail. I needed something, but did not really know what that something was. My troubles had grown beyond my ability to be in control of anything and he was the only one I could think to turn to.

The first thing I told him was, "Bill, I need a friend."

I had not given much thought to my friend's level of faith in the past. He was just a friend who had always been there, but we had not discussed such things before. Listening to Bill encouraged me to have faith and to take new steps in believing and trusting God.

Over the years I had come to think that God wasn't interested in me because of the wrong choices I had made. But now the words Bill spoke meant something special, and when he prayed for me, that did it! Something was different after that and I knew that I had made another choice; I would never be the same again. It was my choice to surrender that day, to give up fighting on my own strength and let God be in control. The most amazing realization is that it was still my choice to surrender—not God's. What a wonderful gift to mankind: the ability to choose.

CLOSER THAN A BROTHER

CHUCK HOLTON
FORMER U.S. ARMY RANGER

Nick was used to being ridiculed for his faith.

After three years in the Marine Corps, it wasn't the first time his principles had gotten in the way of his popularity with the men of the unit. It would have been easy for him to join them on a night of drunken bar-hopping, to just allow himself to be "one of the guys." Nick wanted to be liked as much as the next man, but his Marine Corps training had echoed what the Bible had taught him—that a man's integrity is his most valuable possession.

This trip to the Middle East promised to be tedious. Normally, the sailors enjoyed the ability to e-mail messages from the ship to loved ones back home. On this outing, however, e-mail privileges had been suspended so the troop ship's movements wouldn't become known to the world at large.

One day, however, the burden of loneliness lay especially heavy on Nick's mind and heart, so he went below decks to a quiet place where he liked to pray. "Father," he began, "I feel like I'm fighting this battle alone. It sure would be easier to stay faithful if I had someone to talk to, a friend who could keep me accountable. I don't feel like there's anyone on this boat who believes in You like I do." He went on to ask God to send him a buddy, someone who could keep his faith sharp.

Back in his platoon's berth, not five minutes later, he ran into Sam.

Sam Velasquez had been in the platoon for over a year, but Nick still didn't know much about him. "So why do they call you 'preacher man'?" asked Sam.

Taken somewhat off guard, Nick haltingly told Sam about his faith and watched as an astonished look crossed the younger man's face.

"That's amazing," Sam said. "I've been looking for another Christian to study the Bible with."

Nick was so shocked he almost forgot to offer a quiet prayer of thanks.

Their unit arrived in Kuwait, and Nick and Sam became fast friends as the weeks of waiting wore on. They started studying the Bible together and enjoyed discussing their faith whenever possible. Eventually other marines joined their group, turning more easily toward spiritual things as the war with Iraq loomed closer.

When the fighting finally started, it was almost a blessing. The marines in Nick's unit knew that their only ticket home lay ahead in the city of Baghdad.

Toward the end of March, the unit was given a mission near the town of Nasiriya. They encountered no resistance at first, but after crossing a bridge, the Marine column suddenly came under sniper attack. When Nick stuck his head out of the top of his armored carrier to check on the troops outside, a mortar round hit near him, and a large piece of shrapnel dug into his neck. He sat down heavily inside the transport, stunned. *Lord, please give me the faith to make it through this.*

After a few minutes, Nick was able to remove the shard and stop the bleeding with a compress, not realizing then how close the fragment had come to his carotid artery. A lieutenant stumbled over to Nick's vehicle, bleeding profusely from multiple wounds. Nick turned his attention back to the men outside his vehicle, who were now bearing the brunt of the heavy mortar attack. Forgetting his own injuries, Nick began providing cover fire as the driver started hauling their wounded comrades into the vehicle. Then Nick noticed other vehicles pulling back. "We've got to get out of here!" he yelled, suddenly realizing that their communications must be down.

The enemy fire intensified as they made their way back across the bridge, but then Nick's vehicle was hit again. This time it felt like a mortar round had exploded in his lap.

Everything turned white for Nick. *This is it. I'm not going to make it.*

Somehow, he managed to slide down the side of the now-burning vehicle and run for the safety of a house by the side of the road. Part of him knew that the others in the vehicle hadn't gotten out.

Did Sam make it? Nick fell, and only then did he become aware of the severity of his wounds. He looked down and saw that one of his heels was gone. Then bullets started kicking up sand all around him. Adrenaline made him forget his injuries and somehow he got up and ran to cover.

Some buddies patched him up as best they could, and when reinforcements arrived, Nick was ferried on the back of a tank to the casualty collection point. Corpsmen continued to work over him when his gunny sergeant came by, also injured. He looked at Nick lying on the stretcher and said, "You okay, Elliot?"

"I'm alive," he answered weakly.

"Velasquez got hit too, but he's going to be all right."

An unexpected wave of emotion swept over Nick at the news that his friend was alive. *Thank You, God!* He broke down and started sobbing.

A week and several surgeries later, Nick was recovering in the ICU of a military hospital in Germany. Depression started to creep in, and he began to wish that he was back on the lines with his unit. The medical team had been able to repair the Achilles tendon that had been blown off, but they had to take some skin from his back to close the wound. The doctors told him that he couldn't possibly have run without his Achilles tendon.

But the doctors had never been shot at.

He actually felt a bit guilty for having been injured. He wanted to be there for his men. He was wrestling with those feelings when the physical therapist walked in.

"Someone wants to see you," she said. "Do you feel up to having a visitor?"

Nick wondered who it could be. "Sure."

A few moments later, Velasquez limped into the room, lighting up the room with his smile.

"Sam!"

"Hey there, Corporal. You ready to get back to work yet?"

"Absolutely!"

"The nurse says that in a couple of days you'll be able to move downstairs with the rest of us, unless you'd rather stay here by yourself."

Nick laughed. "I can't wait!"

The two friends were reunited shortly thereafter and stayed together on their return to the States and during their recovery in Bethesda Naval Hospital in Washington, D.C.

The scars they bear will remind everyone they meet of the price of freedom. Nick and Sam, however, see those scars and remember something else. A bond forged by shared wounds and a shared faith—brothers not only in the Marine Corps—but also in God's service.

Even after Sam was discharged, he stayed with Nick's parents so that he could be close enough to visit him until he was also cleared to go home. Both men are expected to recover fully.

∼

Grant us wisdom from Thy mind,
courage from Thine heart,
and protection by Thine hand.
It is for Thee that we do battle,
and to Thee belongs the victor's crown.
For Thine is the kingdom,
and the power and glory forever.

EXCERPT FROM THE SPECIAL FORCES PRAYER

Taps

★ ★ ★

Day is Done
Gone the Sun
From the Lake
From the Hill
From the Sky
Rest in Peace
Soldier Brave
God is Nigh.

BECAUSE
WE CARE

★★★

ONE DAY IN HEAVEN

✯✯✯

Please take a moment to read the verses written on the next page.
Although there are hundreds of verses in the Bible that tell us about
God's love and His gift of salvation, I chose these from the book of
Romans in the New Testament.

I care about what happens to you now, but I care even more about
where you will spend eternity. If you have never asked Jesus Christ to be
your Savior, please consider inviting Him into your life now.

Many years ago I prayed a simple prayer that went something like
this...

Dear Jesus,

I believe You are the Son of God and that You gave Your life
as a payment for the sins of mankind. I believe You rose from the
dead and You are alive today in heaven preparing a place for
those who trust in You.

I have not lived my life in a way that honors You. Please forgive me for my sins and come into my life as Savior and Lord.
Help me grow in Your knowledge and in obedience to You.

Thank You for forgiving me. Thank You for coming into my
life. Thank You for giving me eternal life. Amen.

If you have sincerely asked Jesus Christ to come into your life, He will
never leave you or forsake you. Nothing—absolutely nothing—will be
able to separate you from His love.

God bless you, dear one. I'll look forward to meeting you one day in
heaven.

—Alice Gray

*For all have sinned and fall
short of the glory of God.*

ROMANS 3:23

*For the wages of sin is death, but the gift of God
is eternal life in Christ Jesus our Lord.*

ROMANS 6:23

*But God demonstrates his own love for us in this:
While we were still sinners, Christ died for us.*

ROMANS 5:8

*If you confess with your mouth, "Jesus is Lord"
and believe in your heart that God raised him from
the dead, you will be saved. For it is with your heart
that you believe and are justified, and it is with your
mouth that you confess and are saved.*

ROMANS 10:9–10

*"Everyone who calls on the name
of the Lord will be saved."*

ROMANS 10:13

THE GREATEST ADVENTURE

CHUCK HOLTON
FORMER U.S. ARMY RANGER

Many of the stories in this book have to do with God's protection of soldiers from death or injury. And while prayers for protection are undoubtedly some of the most common, there is a fate worse than death—a wasted life.

William Wallace spoke these words in the movie *Braveheart*: "Every man dies, but not every man truly lives." God put every one of us here on earth at this very time for a very specific reason. He has a mission for you to accomplish, if you are willing.

I can tell you from my experience in the military that being on mission is what every soldier lives for. There's nothing like playing a part in making history. You were custom designed and built to fit perfectly into the plan that God is working out in this world today. By allowing Christ to take charge of your life, you can play a part in *His* story, and I can promise you that there is no more adventurous or fulfilling job on this earth.

Jesus paid the price for every dirty, rotten thing we've ever done. But what He did wasn't just to save us from an eternity apart from God, it was to save us from a meaningless existence here and now.

A vibrant faith brings confidence and security, and these are the makings of a fantastic life. Once you've come to understand this concept, you'll no longer have any reason to fear death, or life, for that matter. For believers, it's a win-win situation! So get on mission—you won't regret it.

~

"'For I know the plans I have for you,'
declares the LORD, 'plans to prosper you
and not to harm you, plans to give you
hope and a future.'"

JEREMIAH 29:11

LIFE IS COMBAT!

The rigor of becoming an Airborne Ranger is exceeded only by the challenge of being one—but those who join their ranks find fulfillment in something bigger than themselves. In the same way, pursuing God's objectives energizes our everyday lives. Former U.S. Army Ranger Chuck Holton shows how God oversees our training and gives each of us specific skills to accomplish the mission He has for us in this great spiritual war. Riveting action and powerful vignettes offer potent spiritual ammunition for the battles of every Christian serving in God's army. Find out what it takes to be a more elite soldier.

ISBN 1-59052-215-X

The Stories for the Heart Series

- More than 5 million sold in series!
- #1-selling Christian stories series!

The Stories for the Heart Series

compiled by Alice Gray

www.storiesfortheheart.com

ACKNOWLEDGMENTS

Every effort has been made to provide proper and accurate source attribution for all selections used in this book. Should any attribution be found to be incorrect, the publisher welcomes written documentation supporting correction for subsequent printings. If you will contact Multnomah Publishers, Inc., Post Office Box 1720, Sisters, Oregon 97759, corrections will be made prior to additional printings. We gratefully acknowledge the cooperation of other publishers and individuals who have granted permission for use of their material.

Notes and acknowledgments are listed by story title in the order they appear in each section of the book. For permission to reprint any of the stories, please request permission from the original source listed below. Where authors have listed websites, we cannot be responsible for the content on those pages. Grateful acknowledgment is made to authors, publishers, and agents who granted permission for reprinting these stories.

PATRIOTISM

"I Pledge Allegiance" by John S. McCain. © 2003. Used by permission of Senator John McCain.

"The Patriot" condensed from *Hope Rising* © 2003 by Kim Meeder. Used by permission of Multnomah Publishers.

"Hidden Heroes" by Ellie Kay. © 2002. Used by permission of the author. Ellie Kay is a best-selling, award-winning author and national speaker. Her book, *Heroes at Home*, was a 2003 Gold Medallion finalist. She is married to an Air Force fighter pilot. The Kays and their seven children make their home in New Mexico.

"A Twenty-One-Day Flag Salute" by David B. Coleman. © 2003. Used by permission of the author. David is a twenty-year Navy veteran and a graduate of Montana Tech with a B.S. in Liberal Studies. He and his family reside in Montana. His son, David, is currently serving in the U.S. Marine Corps.

DEDICATION AND COURAGE

basset hound, Wilson Wellington. She holds her B.A. in communications and political science from the University of Tennessee at Martin. When not writing, Rebeca works in commercial property management.

"On Mission" adapted from *A More Elite Soldier* © 2003 by Chuck Holton. Used by permission of Multnomah Publishers. To schedule Chuck for a speaking event, contact him at soldier@mission4me.com.

"Hog Wild" by Mike Parker. © 2003. Used by permission of the author. Mike Parker is a freelance writer, actor, and director. He served as an officer with the U.S. Army Special Forces (Green Berets). He lives in Nashville with his playwright wife, Paula, and their five children.

"The Soldiers of Bataan" from *Did You Get What You Prayed For?* by Nancy Jo Sullivan and Jane A.G. Kise © 2003. Used by permission of Multnomah Publishers.

"Preserving Memories" by Betty King. © 2003. Used by permission of the author. Betty King is the author of *It Takes Two Mountains to Make a Valley*, a newspaper columnist, and contributor to Chicken Soup series. She writes for Internet sites and is a public speaker. Betty can be reached at www.betty.newsmoose.com or baking2@charter.net.

"Once a Marine, Always a Marine" by Birdie L. Etchison. © 2003. Used by permission of the author.

"From My Tank's Perch" by Tarmo Holma as told to Tricia Goyer. © 2003. Used by permission of the author. Tricia Goyer is the author of *From Dust and Ashes* (Moody Publishing, 2003). Mrs. Goyer interviewed over thirty WWII veterans for this novel and is currently working on a second novel inspired by true events.

"A Soldier's Christmas" from *A More Elite Soldier* © 2003 by Chuck Holton. Used by permission of Multnomah Publishers. To schedule Chuck for a speaking event, contact him at soldier@mission4me.com.

"The Few, the Proud..." by Tom Neven. © 2003. Used by permission of the author. Tom Nevan went on to serve seven years in the Marine Corps, being honorably discharged as a staff sergeant. He lives with his wife and two children in Colorado.

"The Winner" by Martha E. Gorris. © 2003. Used by permission of the author. Martha Gorris is the author of *Held Captive by Futile Thoughts? Break Free!* A CLASS graduate, she speaks to church and women's groups. Fred, her husband, graduated on the dean's list from the Naval Academy in June 1972 and in 1991 reached his dream by taking command of the USS *Fanning*. After a successful tour, with a deployment to the Gulf, he retired as a captain in 1996.

"No Matter How Tough" by Chuck Holton. © 2003. Used by permission of the author. Chuck Holton, a former U.S. Ranger, is the author of *A More Elite Soldier*. To schedule Chuck for a speaking event, contact him at soldier@mission4me.com.

"Delta Alert" by Ellie Kay. © 2002. Used by permission of the author. Ellie Kay is an award-winning, best-selling author and national speaker. Her book, *Heroes at Home,* was a 2003 Gold Medallion finalist. She's a regular on CNBC'S #1 rated *Power Lunch* program. Her diverse titles include *Money Doesn't Grow on Trees* and *The New Bride Guide*. She is married to an active duty air force fighter pilot and they have seven children. To contact Ellie visit her site at www.elliekay.com.

"Brothers" by Gary Walsh. © 2003. Used by permission of the author.

HONOR AND SACRIFICE

"I Came to See My Son's Name" by Jim Schueckler. © 1996. Used by permission of the author. This article was provided courtesy of the Virtual Wall, Vietnam Veterans Memorial. Jim Schueckler was an army helicopter pilot in Vietnam. His experiences as a National Park Service volunteer at the Wall led him to inventing and founding The Virtual Wall ®, www.VirtualWall.org, in 1997.

"The Boys of Iwo Jima" by Michael T. Powers. © 2000. Used by permission of the author. Michael T. Powers, a frequent contributor to the Stories for the Heart series, is a youth pastor, motivational speaker, HS girls coach, and the founder of HeartTouchers.com and Heart4Teens.com. You can preview his book or join the thousands of worldwide readers on his inspirational e-mail list by visiting www.HeartTouchers.com. E-mail: HeartTouchers@aol.com.

"Should the Occasion Arise" from *Into the Teeth of the Tiger* by Donald S. Lopez. © 1997. Used by permission of the author.

"Always Faithful" by Carole Moore. © 2003. Used by permission of the author. Carole Moore's father was in the navy, she is married to a former marine, and she lives three miles from a military base in North Carolina. She wouldn't have it any other way.

"At Graveside" by Charlotte Adelsperger. © 2003. Used by permission of the author. Charlotte Adelsperger is an author and inspirational speaker from Overland Park, KS. She can be reached at Author04@aol.com.

"My Remembrance of Liberation" by John Slatton as told to Tricia Goyer. © 2003. Used by permission of the author. Tricia Goyer is the author of *From Dust and Ashes* (Moody Publishing, 2003). Mrs. Goyer interviewed over thirty WWII veterans for this novel and is currently working on a second novel inspired by true events.

"Open Door to Forgiveness" by Mark Simpson. © 2003. Adapted and used by permission of *Command* magazine, published by Officers' Christian Fellowship, Englewood, CO.

"So Many Dreams" by Diane Dean White. © 2003. Used by permission of the author. Diane Dean White is a freelance writer and former newspaper reporter. She and her husband Stephen are the parents of three grown children, and two grandgals. They make their home on the South Carolina coast where Diane continues her love for writing. Her new book, *Beach Walks*, a collection of heartwarming and inspirational stories, is now available. For more information visit Diane's Web page and outreach for women, called Seeds of Encouragement, www.heartwarmers4u.com/members/?thelamb212.

"A Warrior's Heart" by Jeff Adams. © 2003. Used by permission of the author. Jeff Adams is an award-winning freelance writer and inspirational speaker. He lives in Arizona with his wife, Rosemary, and their daughter, Meaghan. For speaking engagements call 928-753-4530.

"Inferno on Green Ramp" by Mark Lee Walters. © 2003. Adapted and used by permission of *Command* magazine, published by Officers' Christian Fellowship, Englewood, CO.

"The Battle of Leyte" by Curtis Lidbeck. © 2003. Used by permission of the author. Mr. Lidbeck was born in Wisconsin. Served in navy from 1942–1945. Married fifty-eight years. Has five children. Was carpenter at Multnomah Bible College for eighteen years. Resides in Oregon.

"A Warrior's Passing" by Eric Kail. © 2003. Adapted and used by permission of *Command* magazine, published by Officers' Christian Fellowship, Englewood, CO.

"A Sister's Promise" by Harriette Peterson Koopman as told to Connie Pettersen. © 2002. Used by permission of the author. Connie lives in Atkin, MN, and has written for *Cricket, Aglow, War Cry, Women's Touch, Lutheran Woman Today, Witness, Aitkin Independent Age, Duluth News Tribune,* and *Brainerd Daily Dispatch.*

LOVE AND FAMILY

"Mother's Covers" by Bitsy Barnard Craft. © 1994. Used by permission of the author. Bitsy Barnard Craft is a writer and artist. She has authored and illustrated two lines of greeting cards and lives along the banks of the Big Shawnee Creek in Attica, IN.

"God's Perfect Timing" by Bill Dixon as told to Chuck Holton. © 2003. Used by permission of the author. Chuck Holton, a former U.S. Ranger, is the author of *A More Elite Soldier.* To schedule Chuck for a speaking event, contact him at soldier@mission4me.com.

"Faded Photograph" by Bob Henderson. © 1994. Reprinted with permission of the *St. Petersburg Times,* 1994.

"My Turn" by Tom D. Barna. © 2003. Used by permission of the author. Marine Corps Reserve Lieutenant Colonel Tom D. Barna, forty-five-year-old father of three, spent eight months in the Persian Gulf when his son, Alex, was just two. In October, he was called away again from his home in Eagle Lake, MN, just as his son was now twelve.

"Lost and Found" by David B. Coleman. © 2003. Used by permission of the author. David is a twenty-year navy veteran and a graduate of Montana Tech with a B.S. in Liberal Studies. He and his family reside in Montana. His son, David, is currently serving in the U.S. Marine Corps.

"He Is Gone" by Ellie Kay. © 2002. Used by permission of the author. Ellie Kay is an award-winning, best-selling author and national speaker. Her book, *Heroes at Home,* was a 2003 Gold Medallion finalist. She is married to an active duty Air Force fighter pilot. The Kays have seven children.

"A Soldier's Legacy" by Ron Gold. © 2003. Used by permission of the author. Ron writes stories, ethical wills, college entry essays, and personal love stories.

"A Letter Home" by Frank Coffman. © 2003. Used by permission of the author.

"Still, Small Voice" by Robert L. Hilton. © 2003. Used by permission of the author. Robert, a Christian family man, served twenty years in the United States Marine Corps. He spent his year in Vietnam posturing for life, preparing for death, and praying for God's will.

"A Father's Legacy to His Daughter" by Sarah A. McMullen as told to Charlotte Adelsperger. © 2003. Used by permission of the author. Charlotte Adelsperger is an author and inspirational speaker from Overland Park, KS. She can be reached at Author04@aol.com.

"The Rose" by Jennifer Sherwood as told to Bedelia Burchette Murray. © 2003. Used by permission of the author.

"Meeting Father" by Laura Tindal Hulett as told to Lauren Thompson. © 2003. Used by permission of the author.

"For Others First" by Scott Buckingham. © 2003. Used by permission of the author. Air Force Tech Sergeant Scott Buckingham is assigned to the 92nd Aircraft Generation Squadron at Fairchild Air Force Base, Washington. He recently deployed to the Middle East and had to miss his son Kyle's birthday. He has one other child, a daughter.

"Our Christmas Tree" by Irene Costilow. © 2003. Used by permission of the author. Irene has a short story published in *Comfort for the Grieving Heart* by Margolyn Woods and Maureen MacLellan (SunCreek books, 2002).

"Welcome Home" by Alice Gray. © 2003. Based on television and newspaper coverage. Used by permission of the author.

INSPIRATION

"The Prayer Card" by Charlotte Adelsperger. © 2003. Used by permission of the author. Charlotte Adelsperger is an author and inspirational speaker from Overland Park, KS. She can be reached at Author04@aol.com.

"The Photo that Answered a Prayer" by Andrew Knox. © 2003. Reprinted with permission of The 700 Club/Christian Broadcasting Network. All rights reserved.

"Grateful Warrior" by Chuck Holton. © 2003. Used by permission of the author. Chuck Holton, a former U.S. Ranger, is the author of *A More*

lished books with the *Time/Life* magazine and *Reader's Digest* publications of his "Lords Prayers." Visit www.davidredding.com for ordering information.

FAITH ON THE FRONT LINES

"Baptism in the Sand" by Lynne M. Thompson. © 2003. Used by permission of the author. Lynne M. Thompson may be reached at www.kidfishy.com.

"Sixty Days in the Wilderness" by Chuck Holton. © 2003. Used by permission of the author. Chuck Holton, a former U.S. Ranger, is the author of *A More Elite Soldier.* To schedule Chuck for a speaking event, contact him at soldier@mission4me.com.

"The Helmet and the Sword" by Marilyn K. McAuley. © 2003. Used by permission of the author.

"Lesson from Desert Storm" by Danny Smith as told to Kayleen Reusser. © 2003. Used by permission of the author. Kayleen is a freelance writer with over four hundred published articles. She is married, has three children, and works at Taylor University–Ft. Wayne. Kayleen's husband is in the Air National Guard and her son will be a cadet at the Air Force Academy fall 2003.

"The Hand of God" by LeRoy "Pete" Petersohn as told to Tricia Goyer. © 2003. Used by permission of the author. Tricia Goyer is the author of *From Dust and Ashes* (Moody Publishing, 2003). Mrs. Goyer interviewed over thirty WWII veterans for this novel and is currently working on a second novel inspired by true events.

"God Is My Autopilot" by Chuck Holton. © 2003. Used by permission of the author. Chuck Holton, a former U.S. Ranger, is the author of *A More Elite Soldier.* To schedule Chuck for a speaking event, contact him at soldier@mission4me.com.

"Every Man a Warrior" by Dave Meurer. © 2002. Used by permission of the author. Dave Meurer is the author of *Stark Raving Dad! A Fairly Functional Guide to Fatherhood.*

"God's Army Medal" by Bill Gothard. © 2003. Used by permission of the author. Information for this story was received from Mike Shellman and his wife.

★★★

For information about Alice Gray: www.alicegray.com